For Nicole,

Here's an artist's date (maybe several) ready when you are! Enjoy.

Thank you for enriching my life with your art and thoughts shared.

Susan Jacobi

2/21/00

Endangered
Pleasures

Barbara Holland

Endangered
Pleasures

In Defense of Naps, Bacon,
Martinis, Profanity, and
Other Indulgences

Little, Brown and Company
Boston New York London

First Edition

"Birds," "Air," "Spring," "Seasonal Food," and "Spending the Summer" first appeared in *Country Journal*.

Library of Congress Cataloging-in-Publication Data
Holland, Barbara.
    Endangered pleasures : in defense of naps, bacon, martinis, profanity, and other indulgences / Barbara Holland. — 1st ed.
        p.   cm.
    ISBN 0-316-37057-6
    1. United States — Social life and customs — 1971–   I. Title.
E169.04.H64   1995
973.92 — dc20
                                                                94-39087

10

MV-NY

Designed by Barbara Werden
Illustrations by Bob Barner

Printed in the United States of America

*In memory of my aunt Peggy, who
enjoyed every minute*

Contents

Preface

SUBTLY, in little ways, joy has been leaking out of our lives. Almost without a struggle, we have let the New Puritans take over, spreading a layer of foreboding across the land until even ignorant small children rarely laugh anymore. Pain has become nobler than pleasure; work, however foolish or futile, nobler than play; and denying ourselves even the most harmless delights marks the suitably somber outlook on life.

It's an easy trap to fall into. Somehow bad news is easier to believe, more important, than good. Joyful people singing of blue skies always sound slightly simple-minded; the prophets of doom sound so much better educated, so much more likely to be right, and when they threaten us with cancer, rape, global warming, gridlock, AIDS, war, famine, and pestilence, we listen closely and believe. The small pleasures of the ordinary day come to seem almost contemptible, and glance off us lightly. By bedtime they've vanished, lost among the ominous headlines, rude taxi drivers, and tight shoes looming in memory.

Part of this is genetic programming. Back in the dawn of things, those who dawdled on the path smelling the flowers and smiling at the sunshine didn't last long enough to hand down their genes. The genes that traveled farthest were those of the most pessimistic, the most resistant to pleasures, the most alert to flies in their soup, tigers on the trail. They invented the angriest gods and prepared for the most menacing neighbors. Gloomy and suspicious, they slept with one eye open.

We are their heirs. Scientific tests are proving that we notice and remember dark words more sharply than bright ones. They weigh more in our minds, as tigers weighed more than flowers.

We may be overdoing it. Certainly we suffer more from stress, high blood pressure, insomnia, indigestion, and dark premonitions than other animals whose lives are more perilous than ours. It may not even be a sign of high intelligence; the clever dolphin, in spite of tuna nets, seems to celebrate all day long.

Americans in particular have always been wary of pleasure. When we ponder the great question of life, how shall we spend our days on earth, enjoying ourselves as much as possible is not a respectable answer to come up with. "The pursuit of happiness" isn't expected to mean *fun*. Indeed, many of our ancestors came over here specifically to escape from all that post-Cromwellian singing and dancing, drinking and wenching, ruffles and ribbons and bows. They *hated* fun.

Other ancestors came over because they could make more money here than back home, which is perfectly reasonable but not very merry.

From time to time, because even Americans are human, the country is shaken by a fit of pleasure. Sometimes it's regional: westering pioneers left Victorian disapproval behind and danced around the campfire; even the girls, escaping supervision on horseback, were allowed to have fun. Back East, in the 1890s, the rich ran amok and lavished amazing sums on balls and banquets, yachts and racehorses; newspapers devoted whole issues to their parties.

After a brief pause for the Great War, the 1920s roared in, escorted by Prohibition. The gloomy reign of Cromwell produced the hilarity of the Restoration; the clammy hand of Prohibition squeezed forth the merriment of the twenties. Everyone carried hip flasks and drove around in convertibles singing funny songs. They danced all night. Theaters and movie houses rattled with laughter and a generation of wits wrote and uttered their immortal lines.

The party collapsed overnight, to be followed by the Depression of the thirties, the war of the forties, and the daunting respectability of the fifties.

For a brief while in the late sixties and early seventies, a highly visible minority embraced artificially enhanced pleasures, and this confirmed the disapproval of the rest of the country. Drugs were worse, morally worse, than drink. Drinking too much could be seen as either a recognized illness or a sign of unhappiness; the drinker drank to forget his troubles, while the pot smoker smoked simply for fun. He lolled around with his friends stringing beads and appreciating the goodness of life and not getting any work done, and this was unproductive, the cardinal American sin, and gave fun an even worse name.

During the hangover years of the seventies the pot smokers got older and their parents couldn't afford to support them any longer. A handful of them retreated into the mountains of North Carolina to make dulcimers, but this was more protest than pleasure.

Sex, cheaper than drugs and less time-consuming, enjoyed nearly a decade as life's main delight, but it turned out not to be as lighthearted as we'd hoped and presently caved in under the brutal weight of medical advice.

Blinking, we wandered into the eighties, which brought us AIDS and cholesterol and the message that pleasure was not just disreputable, it was downright life-threatening. The scuttling of sex as the last private, independent pleasure left the field clear for toilsome virtue.

Now in the nineties we're left to wring joy from the absence of joy, from denial, from counting grams of fat, jogging, drinking only bottled water and eating only broccoli. The rest of the time we work. A recent study informs us that Americans in 1994 worked 158 hours, or roughly a month, longer than we did in 1974.

This use of our days remains a mystery to countries where people like to loll around in the sunshine drinking vin rosé and chatting with their friends, but then, those places have always been a mystery to us, too.

Our only permissible enjoyments now are public, official, and commercially regulated, as in Disney World, casinos, shopping, television, organized sport, and rock concerts. As long as somebody somewhere is making money out of us, we're useful to the economy, even patriotic: we're allowed to pay admission and play in the theme park.

To make sure we aren't having any casual, private fun, the contemporary wisdom has withdrawn a lot of our older pleasures — chicken gravy, long summer vacations, cigarettes, martinis, sleeping late — and replaced them with fitness and gloom.

Life in the nineties is no laughing matter. Imagine a serious grown-up like Beethoven today writing his "Ode to Joy" — a tune I heard most recently as background to a television commercial. The commercial was on choosing the right hospital for heart surgery.

Joy, modern-American-style.

Perhaps it's a good time to reconsider pleasure at its roots. Changing out of wet shoes and socks, for instance. Bathrobes. Yawning and stretching. Real tomatoes. The magic day in January when it's clearly, plainly, joyfully no longer quite dark at five in the afternoon. Waking up in the morning and then going back to sleep again. The cold and limey rattle of a vodka-tonic being walked across the lawn. Finishing our tax returns. The smells of the morning paper, cut grass, and old leather jackets. Finding a taxi in a downpour; clean sheets; singing to ourselves in the car. Sitting by the fire picking sticktights off the dog. All the available gentle nourishments of the ordinary day. Properly respected, maybe they can lighten our anxious load.

Indeed, pleasure may be almost as good for our health as broccoli; chemists tell us that happy people produce endorphins and enkephalins, brain chemicals that improve T-cell production and thus enhance immunity to cancer, heart disease, and infections.

Let us then strive to be merry. Gloom we have always with us, a rank and sturdy weed, but joy requires tending. Pleasure itself is endangered.

> Give strong drink unto him that is ready to perish, and wine unto those who be of heavy hearts.
>
> Let him drink, and forget his poverty, and remember his misery no more.
>
> PROVERBS 31:6, 7

Endangered
Pleasures

Waking Up

OBVIOUSLY the best possible time to wake up is in the June of our tenth year, on the first day of summer vacation. Failing that, another good time is in winter, facing east on the only bright morning in a long string of dark ones.

I did it recently, while visiting a country friend. She'd thoughtfully put me to bed in a tiny southeastern room with deep windows, so the bed was at sill level, and I woke up covered all over with the low yellow winter sunlight, as if Zeus had descended in a shower of gold and I would presently give birth to a minor goddess. Never underestimate the power of daylight in December.

In a window is a good place to wake up. For years in the city I lived in a small old rowhouse with low windows and slept at the windowsill, twelve feet straight up from the sidewalk. In the morning I could check the day from my pillow; the state of the sky; whether the people across the street had raised their upstairs blinds yet; whether the pedestrians wore their coats open or buttoned tightly. A window is the world's threshold, or vestibule. Some misguided hearties claim to enjoy waking up outdoors, completely *in* the world, participants instead of spectators, but this is too much responsibility for me at that hour. Too much sky. The room around us is our cave and protection — our sleep, so to speak — and the window is the world and the day ahead, or the waking state, and we lie there balanced at the transition between them. This is a good and gentle way to reenter the daily life.

Which brings up the subject of how to wake painlessly at the appointed hour. The same country friend, who has virtuously given up eating eggs, keeps chickens around anyway because she likes to hear the roosters crowing. A rooster is the classic and one of the pleasanter ways to be dragged out of sleep, or would be if he were more reliable. Some roosters don't crow until noon, and then keep it up till dinnertime. Most of them, in May and June, carry on hysterically at the first gray of dawn, which is no time for sane folk to be abroad. You can't count on a rooster, and many of us aren't in a position to keep one in the apartment anyway. We have alarm clocks, or clock radios.

Those who are seriously anti-pleasure go for a loud, angry, relentless ringing or buzzing sound to rend the soft rosy fabric of sleep and yank them into the day. This satisfies their masochism and leaves their nerves twitching till noon. A modern variation on this produces a thin electronic whine that can easily be silenced by the sleeper and then, five minutes later, another, more insistent whine. This has the advantage of letting us slip back into sleep — one of life's purer pleasures — over and over, with the disadvantage of being a thoroughly mean and hateful sound. Why not bells, for heaven's sake? Distant church bells, or chimes, or a far-off trumpet solo, or a mockingbird, or a fife-and-drum corps, or even a rooster, reliably prerecorded? Too pleasant, I suppose; inconsistent with the stern realities of the day ahead. Besides, we might just lie there happily listening to them for hours.

We might, if we've prudently supplied ourselves with an attractive warm body in the bed beside us, be inspired by bells and roosters to make love instead of leaping out of bed, and having done so, drift sweetly back to sleep.

The alternative to alarms is the clock radio, set the night before to whichever station we choose to reach into our naked, bemused, and vulnerable inner selves and snatch us forth like a snail winkled from its shell. Set it to the wrong number and heavy-metal rock will blast you across the room at dawn and leave you trembling like a leaf, unable even to pour coffee. On the other hand, a symphony may not do the trick at all. Glance around the concert hall. Many people would actually rather sleep to classical music, even sitting upright, than to silence. I tried the all-news station for a while, but this wasn't quite satisfactory either. A voice, usually a stern and solemn, rather biblical voice, pounced on me, either from on high or from under the bed, bearing inscrutable messages: ". . . thirteen killed and twenty-three injured" or ". . . in the right-hand lane. Traffic is backed up to Swedesford Road in Centerville. . . ." This always snapped me to attention, bewildered: *Why is he telling me? Is it my fault? My responsibility? What must I do? Who is he and how did he get into my room?*

The only truly pleasurable answer is to sleep until we float gradually, swinging in and out of consciousness, to the surface, and lie there smiling at the ceiling, afloat under weightless goose down in winter, a soft white cotton sheet in summer, until it seems good to get out of bed. This is a joy we should seize whenever possible, making a conscious effort not to think about money or errands or anything at all until we're actually up and at the coffee pot. Some people — I was married to one of them — find this so enjoyable as to be quite viciously decadent, and they spring up at once, checking the clock and berating themselves, and rush to the shower, though they have nothing at all to do until Monday morning.

The rest of us count not getting out of bed as the best part of waking up.

Coffee

INSTANT coffee is the measure of America's anti-pleasure bias. Since it's no faster or easier to make than real coffee, it apparently exists only as a kind of punishment, a ritual morning flagellation of the senses, to ready us for whatever nastiness the day may bring. It also seems to be a measure of our vulnerability to advertising: relentless campaigns assure us that, not only is the stuff drinkable, it's actually *good*, at least their brand of it, and one even claims that many famous restaurants slip it to their customers, who are delighted with its "richness" and amazed to hear it's instant. To anyone who has ever tasted the wretched liquid, this is arrant nonsense. It tastes no more like coffee than like orange juice, and its sour chemical smell can bring the thirstiest morning mouth to a dead stop three inches from the cup's rim. The perfume of real coffee is a major component of its satisfaction; it permeates the rooms, rousing sleepers with glad anticipation. The miasma of instant coffee, luckily, remains hovered over the cup and offends only the disappointed would-be drinker.

Getting out of bed to find real coffee already made is a civilized way to begin the day and an incentive to fling off the covers and rise. It's an easy pleasure, requiring only a coffeemaker with a timer, to be filled with water and coffee the night before, when your mind is clear and your hand steady. Purists object, claiming the water should be freshly drawn and the coffee freshly ground, but few of us are such exacting gourmets at dawn. Hair spiky, eyes crumbed, we grope our way to the kitchen and lo, there it is, the earth mother, the bountiful friend, the kindly kitchen genie waiting, hot and fragrant. All we need to do is lay our hands on a cup.

For you instant-coffee drinkers who claim you use the savage brew because you need only a single cup, the answer is equally simple. Find yourself a plastic coffee-filter holder, probably somewhere near the coffee counter in the supermarket, and some appropriately small paper filters. In the morning, boil the water as usual, and while it's coming to a boil, place the holder, with filter, over an empty mug. Put a scoopful of ground coffee in the filter. Pour boiling water into it. This is in no respect more difficult or time-consuming than stirring chemical powders into the same mug, and the result is pleasure as compared to pain.

For those who go visiting overnight at the homes of benighted friends with only instant coffee in their cupboards, the holder, filters, and a sandwich bag full of coffee are easily packed and transported. If the friends take umbrage, tell them your doctor says instant coffee aggravates your ulcer, which it almost certainly does. Then offer them a sip. Pleasures shared are pleasures heightened — not to mention the happiness of showing others that ours are more refined than theirs.

Breakfast

T HE breakfast hour is no time for creative experimentation, which is why everyone's more or less content to eat the same breakfast five or six days a week, while a dinner repeated even once is an outrage. Breakfast was never really supposed to be a pleasure anyway; it was nutrition, and something of a moral litmus test for the lady of the house. For generations the word was preceded — sometimes reproach-fully — by the adjectives "hot" and "nourishing," which were syn-onymous. Toasted bread, for instance, was a proper, if minimal, breakfast, while a slice of the same stuff untoasted wasn't much better morally than a Hershey bar, and a crying shame to the mother or wife who permitted it.

Breakfast has changed its clothes completely in the past decade; "nutritious" has been replaced by "low-fat," and "hot" means sinful, as in eggs. Dry cereal moistened with skim milk is now the politi-cally correct morning meal, and everything that cried out for butter, including oatmeal, has been banished. In television commercials, couples who presumably do their grocery shopping separately ar-gue about the comparative virtues of their respective cereals. "You say it's ninety-eight-percent fat-free?" they ask incredulously. "Hey, let me taste that!"

Conveniently, this revolution coincided with the rush of women into the workforce; the lady of the house who used to be out in the kitchen timing eggs and buttering toast for her family is now spong-ing her pinstriped suit and frantically repacking her briefcase while the family dumps its own cereal into bowls.

Here the new Spartanism has its advantages. For one thing, it elevates a number of previously routine matters into the realm of illicit thrills. What was once an ordinary, underappreciated break-fast — two eggs over easy, bacon, and a well-buttered English muf-fin, for instance — now packs the guilty wallop of adultery, or starting the day with a slug of Napoleon brandy. In order to extract its maximum enjoyment, many people eat the approved horse chows during the working week and then celebrate Sunday morn-ings with a groaning board of rosy ham slices, crisply browned little sausages, platters mounded with bacon and home-fried potatoes, bowls of eggs scrambled with cream. Greedily they survey the land-scape of cholesterol and lap their napkins in glad anticipation. Only the virtuous can truly appreciate sin.

To my way of thinking, the ideal breakfast is probably a glass of cold champagne and a perfectly ripe pear, perhaps with a spoonful of caviar eaten straight from the jar. This should be served with sunlight spreading across the table, or, better, outdoors on a balcony or flagstone patio, in the company of a single well-behaved honeybee and someone with whom you're madly in love.

When you've finished the champagne, it's correct to go back, holding hands, to bed.

This doesn't happen often. Still, it's a vision to hold and savor in the mind while we spoon up the Cheerios; imagined joys never get rained on.

Exercise

ONCE, not needing to exercise in order to survive was a privilege and the hallmark of gentlefolk, who were identified by their soft white hands and merely vestigial muscles. Well rested, heartily fed, and flushed with excellent port, many of these sluggards lived to an overripe old age, annoying their heirs, while for those who exercised all day life was nasty, brutish, and mercifully short. We have failed to profit by their example. We have, as a nation, embraced voluntary, non-essential exercise.

For those of us left behind by the new wave, yawning, stretching, and reaching for the coffee cup are quite enough activity to liven up the muscles for the day. For the au courant, however, only violence will suffice. They rush out into the humid smog or the icy darkness and run as if demons were after them, coming back purplish, gasping, and awash in self-satisfaction and sweat. Sometimes, to set the gold seal on their virtue, they suffer from pulled hamstrings, tendinitis, shin-splints, and muggers. They support a whole new branch of science called "sports medicine."

Smugness is one of life's basic joys, and for the altruistic exerciser there's also the amusement he gives to onlookers and the rest of the family, who sit there dry and comfortable, reading the funnies, buttering their muffins, and rejoicing in sloth. The family cat, who stays fit as a fiddle on twenty-two hours of sleep a day, stretches luxuriously, smiles, and gets on with his nap.

As an extra delight, I'm told the fleet-footed sometimes enjoy what's called a "runner's high," a fit of euphoria vouchsafed to those who have pushed it clear to the edge of cardiac arrest. God knows I'm in no position to report on this personally, but it sounds to me like the diver's problem, "rapture of the deep," which involves nitrogen poisoning or oxygen starvation or something. Pleasure is where you find it.

The new, enlightened exercise is governed by a new, improved set of rules, mysterious to the outsider.

First, if you're having fun, as in dancing or skiing, no benefits accrue. No proper runner has ever been seen to smile; no proper lap-swimmer dangles at pool's edge sipping a cool drink and chatting with friends. Exercise, to qualify at all, must be lonely, painful, humorless, and boring.

Second, it must produce no useful effect on anything except your muscles or, some say, your cardiovascular condition. Mowing the lawn, sweeping the floor, and toiling up the basement stairs with a basket of laundry are useless because of the irrelevant purpose involved; rowing a boat gets you, with luck and a favorable current, from point A to point B and is therefore not exercise. For exercise, there are machines (called "equipment") that simulate mowing, rowing, sweeping, and stair-climbing, and these machines perform miracles for the body because they were designed to do nothing else; however long you labor at them, the laundry still languishes in the dryer and sassafras saplings sprout in the lawn. Perhaps you can hire someone to deal with them, thus doubling your outlay.

Third, exercise should cost money. Money proves that you're really serious about this body business, and the body, flattered, responds. There are dues to pay at the gyms and spas and pools, and the truly serious buy their own machinery. Friends of mine replaced their living-room couch with a rowing machine, most wondrously awkward to sit on. For years my brother stabled a sort of steel giraffe, called a NordicTrack, in the guest room. He was never seen to operate the thing, but it was useful for hanging up one's jacket or drying one's underwear, and effective in breaking the toes of guests trying to find the light switch in the dark. Presently it disappeared. I don't know how; it was much too heavy to steal or throw away. It had cost a fortune.

Even the runners, fleeing like purse-snatchers through the morning streets, have spent money. They carry patented weights in both hands, wear special running shorts or suits, dam the sweat from their eyes with special headbands, and buy shoes so expensive that simply contemplating them on the closet floor improves one's muscle tone.

Adhere to the rules and you too may find happiness. As I said, I'm no authority on the joy of exercising; for some of us it lies more in the breach than in the observance. We can stroll to the window with our coffee cup, gaze down as the virtuous go laboring past, and enjoy a wholesome flush of pleasure at not being numbered among them.

Showering, Bathing

EVERY morning the proper American stands under a heavy spray of running water and soaps off the dust and sweat of the previous day or the morning's three-mile run. This is a duty, not a pleasure. The urgency of the pounding water discourages loitering and, since all the other proper people in the household want to do the same thing at roughly the same time, there may be a line forming. The only joy involved comes afterward, with the faint private satisfaction of being clean and socially acceptable, but since as proper Americans we get that way every morning, this glow dims with repetition, and besides, we weren't that foul to begin with. Had our hair been caked with dried mud, had we been truly disgustingly grimed and odorous, like a coal miner or a linebacker in the rainy season, merely getting clean would be a joy, but for most of us it's pretty routine.

From time to time the very rich go to a spa, where they spend serious money for, as far as I can tell, the privilege of taking a comfortable bath, a pleasure once freely available to all. If you bathe in a spa, you're doing it for your health's sake, which makes it virtuous; back when ordinary people could do it at home, it was pure enjoyment, like smoking pot, and wicked. It was too deliciously decadent, too sybaritic, too easily indulged in by the uneducated, who can't handle that much luxury. Righteously, the American designers and manufacturers took the comfortable bathtub off the market entirely and replaced it with the device we all now own, though rarely use.

Those who have bathed in Europe, or lived in poverty in ancient, unmodernized apartments, remember the real bathtub. It was long and deep and narrow, and made of cast iron, so that the water stayed at its original temperature for a sinfully long time. The back sloped at an angle perfectly calibrated to support the human frame. The bather stepped into this iron lounge chair and reclined chin-deep in water, warm in winter, cool in summer, and soaked. The water could be infused with bubbles, or soothing herbs or oils. A washcloth could be folded across the forehead. The cares of the day — bathing was an evening, not morning, occupation — melted. The eyes closed automatically with luxury, and sometimes the bather fell asleep, slid under, and drowned, happy to the last.

Almost no one falls asleep in a shower or, for that matter, a modern bathtub, designed to be even less body-friendly than the coach seats on a plane. Those who persevere these days in trying to re-create the custom must sit bolt upright, submerged only from the waist down, chilly or sweaty from there on up, wondering why they bothered. If they try to recline against the straight, hard, unwelcoming back, they're supporting half their body weight on their necks, in danger of developing whiplash. The flimsy walls of the tub let the water reach room temperature, too cold or too warm, almost instantly. Besides, the water lies wastefully in all the wrong places, mostly to the sides and rear of the bather instead of wrapping him or her to the collarbone in comfort.

Some of life's pleasures lie ready to hand every day; some persist only in the memory of senior citizens, but such pure joys as a bath are well worth remembering, celebrating, and enjoying in the imagination if not in the flesh.

(While we're here, we should call your attention to the rest of the bathroom. People don't usually gather together rejoicing about the subject, but everyone privately agrees that a hearty and effortless bowel movement is one of the morning's significant satisfactions. It represents casting off the burdens of the previous day and rising up to begin the new one unencumbered by the past, and it deserves a little quiet celebration.)

The Morning Paper

SOME few of us can arrange to have the paper delivered to the doorstep, where we can reach around and snake it in while wearing a bathrobe, or nothing at all. This is a fine thing, but growing rarer. Suburbanites could once rely on a freckled teenager who rode by on his bike and pitched the paper against the door with a solid, announcing thump, taking understandable pride in his aim. In most suburbs he's been replaced by an anonymous adult in a car who drops the news in the hedge or the gutter or under a bush; in order to find and retrieve it the homeowner needs to be fully dressed, because it may take a long time and it's probably pouring rain. In the city, doorstepped papers tend to get swiped for resale on the nearest street corner. In the country they're put in a box out on the paved road and you need a car to go get them. However, the paper at the door is a happy luxury where it can be managed.

The paper introduces the day in a more manageable way than radio or television; we can take it at our own pace, sieving out what we want to know and ignoring what we don't. It's a physical, rather than electronic, presence, and its scent and feel are quietly satisfying without jarring our frail morning senses. Those who believe in jump-starting their days can spring straight into the front page, as into an icy pond, with the revolutions and bomb threats and budget crises and drive-by shootings, while those who prefer easing into the world gradually, dipping the toe in first, so to speak, can begin at the back with the funnies, the horoscope, and Ann Landers.

The paper read on the subway or commuter train is all right but more utilitarian than the paper at the breakfast table. By the time you're on the train the day is launched, the mind already distracted and less open to enjoyment. The fullest flavor of a paper is distilled over breakfast.

Clothes

I F we never wore any clothes, we'd look almost exactly the
same every day. Oh, the sharp-eyed might notice, over time,
an extra bulge here or a sag there, perhaps the odd strand of
gray in the chest-hair, but basically we wouldn't change
much: skin is skin.

Long ago, for purely practical reasons, we took to wearing a bit
of something over the skin, a grass loincloth, maybe, or a scrap of
tiger's hide. These also tended to look the same every day, except
for the grass getting dryer and the tiger stripes fading in the sun.
When they wore out completely we got new ones, and I suppose
others noticed and commented, and gradually the idea of variety
took hold. We could look different from day to day; turn up on
Saturday night in something flashier than Tuesday's bearskin. At-
tract some attention around here.

The opposite sex began to take an interest and it was nice, back
before we could do much to improve our ears and noses, to improve the over-all impression with garments and bangles. Looking
better cheered us up. The clothes, once we'd fastened them on,
became our very selves, and mighty handsome we were, too.

Civilization pressed forward. Clothes got fancier for those who
could afford them fancy, and became a status symbol. You'll notice
in friezes all those ordinary Egyptians wearing nothing but identical knee-length wrap skirts, while King Tut's most casual garments
were so glorious they made you squint.

The great thing about fancy, obviously expensive clothes was and is their portability; you might own the world's most elaborate castle packed with priceless works of art, but you can't drag it with you when you go to a party; people have to take your word for it. Clothes, on the other hand, always come along to explain your wealth and power and social importance to strangers.

Clothes can also make, as the copywriters say, a statement, in addition to our net worth. They can be used to proclaim who we uniquely and individually are, but this is rare and considered eccentric. A printed T-shirt is as close as most of us come, and everyone reading it knows that ours is hardly the only shirt urging the world to legalize marijuana or visit Myrtle Beach; it merely identifies us as one of a group or clan that shares those sentiments.

We like to belong to groups, and group identity, at least for men, has come to be the principal purpose of getting dressed in the morning. Consider the armies of rebellious young in the sixties, identically clad in the frazzled jeans that marked them as anarchically unique. Consider soldiers, policemen, Roman senators, and lawyers, all happy as clams to be dressed en masse. The businessman's scope for distinction is scarcely wider than the soldier's. The pleasure of uniformity is modern man's thin substitute for the old, sensuous, creative pleasure of choosing clothes.

Not surprisingly, women spend some of their happiest hours shopping for clothes, while men drag themselves forth only reluctantly when it's time to replace the navy suit with another navy suit. The joys of variety and self-expression are for the moment an almost exclusively female prerogative. Men, understandably envious, jeer at it.

It wasn't always so. In the seventeenth century Samuel Pepys gloated shamelessly over the delivery of each new garment, and reveled in its fashionable touches, its lining, its decorative slashes, the richness of its fabric, and debated with himself where and when to wear it first, for maximum impact. No conquest of a pretty actress earned as much ink as the arrival of a new waistcoat.

Stroll through any portrait gallery and admire the gents' finery; one can hardly suppose they got dressed with modern indifference, not in those velvets and laces. Even our own William Penn, and him a Quaker, galloped around Philadelphia with his trademark bright blue silk sash a-fluttering. Martin Van Buren, our otherwise undistinguished eighth president, strolled Washington in a velvet-collared coat, a lace-trimmed orange necktie, white duck trousers, and yellow kid gloves. The most dashing of our Civil War officers, Colonel Mosby, swooped down on his famous raids splendid in a scarlet-lined cape and a hat with an arching ostrich-feather plume.

You can't tell me they didn't all take a natural and harmless delight in putting their clothes on. No man, especially no Quaker, troubles to wrap himself in a blue silk sash unless the touch and sight of it pleases him deeply, and surely it's a pity that our current conventions have extinguished this light in the lives of half the population, leaving them cranky and morose as you see them to-day. A sparkle has faded from their eyes and a spring deserted their step. We've turned back the clock to prehistory; men might as well be naked for all the sensual pleasure and variety they get from their clothes. A Hawaiian-print shirt on Saturday is small consolation for charcoal gray all week.

It's discriminatory to deprive one sex of innocent joys freely indulged in by the other. Bring back, I say, lace cuffs and velvet breeches, silk sashes and hats with plumes, scarlet and royal blue and touches of gold, ruffles at the throat and buckles on the shoes. Then and only then will we see world affairs take a turn for the better and meetings of high-level officials twinkle merrily along, with much admiring of cut and fingering of fabrics, with an exchange of the addresses of hatters and shoemakers and general goodwill all around.

Besides, just think how it will dress up the streets and brighten the view of, say, Wall Street at lunch hour.

Cigarettes

NOW that we've all been told half to death of the medical horrors lying in wait for smokers, those who were never lured into the filthy habit gaze in slack-jawed amazement at those who were: How could we possibly have done such a disgusting and dangerous thing? Whatever possessed us? And not just once, mind you, but over and over, for years. Decades. In heaven's name, why?

Well, it's time somebody explained. No, we weren't attempting suicide, or deliberately trying to stunt our unborn children or poison the bystanders. We did it because it was fun. It felt good. It felt good like scratching an itch, or stretching, or biting a grain of caviar, or having your back rubbed, or taking off tight shoes.

There, I said it.

Cigarettes tasted good. Their flavor mixed happily with other tastes; apples, cold beer, after-dinner coffee.

They were sexy. The shared cigarette. The compelling gaze half masked by lazy bluish veils of smoke. The courtship gesture of the smoothly produced flame for her waiting cigarette, with an exchange of meaningful looks. The sensual implications of lighting someone's cigarette between one's own lips and then, slowly, handing it over. The sweet camaraderie of the after-sex cigarettes, the pair of identical small orange lights signaling each other like fireflies in the dark bedroom, their glow a wordless message of satisfaction that replaced speech, compliments, promises. It softened the abrupt departures of both parties into separate sleep; "I am here," it said, and "So am I."

The passing of cigarettes leaves all phases of romance impoverished.

One cigarette was worth a thousand words. The infinite inflections of producing and lighting it, inhaling and exhaling, spoke volumes about personality, mood, intention. Many famous actors owed their reputations to cigarette technique. The half-smoked butt flung down, or flicked over the shoulder, or ground out very carefully on the sole of the boot meant that the time for negotiation was over and the action would begin. The cigarette pause, in which the protagonist, halfway through a sentence or before answering a question, takes out and lights a cigarette, repays years of study by cinema buffs.

Men, notoriously shy of personal conversation, relied heavily on them. A group of men could gather and stand around and smoke together, enjoying each other's company, without the need of speech. Now smokeless, they're left just standing there like an arrangement of stones, hands dangling, until embarrassment breaks up the group.

The tobacco offer was a gesture of peace, as it was among American Indians. One took out a cigarette, then offered the pack to another, saying "Cigarette?" The other might accept, putting him or her subtly in the first person's debt and boding well for the upcoming transaction, or refuse, implying unwillingness to cooperate; coolness if not downright hostility.

The cigarette relieved tension, and became the traditional last rite and final perk before the firing squad.

It gave us a chance to think. Faced with a sudden decision or unexpected proposal or proposition, it delayed response by a crucial thirty seconds or so while we extracted one from pack or case, considered it, lit up, and thoughtfully inhaled.

After the battle, after the surgery or the car accident or the lost child found, the cigarette clutched in shaking hands gentled down our panic in its silken cradle of smoke.

Cigarettes were a social crutch, offering shy people something to do with their hands, along with welcome moments when they weren't expected to talk.

They were the seal of a job accomplished, especially a physical job. Having finished painting the porch furniture or planting the daylilies or waxing the car or scaling a cliff, we stood back for a long, satisfying moment to admire what we'd done and smoke the cigarette of reward.

They gave us something to fidget with while waiting for the phone to ring, or the bus to come, or the baby to be born. Something to do during those inevitable blank spots in the conversation. Something to distract the whisper of hunger when we were far from lunch. Tic-Tacs and worry beads are not the same.

For the last smokers, as their numbers dwindled the private-club atmosphere strengthened. The gallant little band, half frozen in an alley behind the office, half choked in a sealed hallway or smoking car, huddled under the marquee at intermission, or meeting by chance, led by the scent of smoke, in a damp, foggy garden halfway through a dinner party, were immediate companions in sin. Wordlessly, they shared mixed feelings of shame at their bondage and a kind of defiant pride in their stubbornness.

The last smokers know the joy of walking into someone's office after a long, smoke-free, corporate day and inhaling the sudden friendly reek of ashtray: liberty at last.

They recognize each other by smell. Like Henry V, a smoker meeting other smokers "bids them good morrow with a modest smile,/And calls them brothers, friends and countrymen."

Besides the human comradeship, the cigarettes themselves were company. All longtime smokers who have given up report the pervasive sadness of their absence, as of the death of a friend. The little white companions of our whole adult lives, more faithful and durable than many a spouse, are missing from our pockets, vanished from our desks and bedside tables. We feel abandoned and diminished.

If you had to ask, it's hard to explain. They're no longer a legitimate pleasure, but they were a pleasure once. We may have been stupid to smoke, but we didn't smoke from sheer stupidity; we smoked because we liked it.

Working

THE joy of being at work isn't fully savored until we've been unemployed for a time — and, of course, vice versa. The human mind, bewildered by imagination and free will and anxiety and other purely human problems, longs for order. The job supplies it. Perhaps we work for lunatics in a state of constant chaos, but still employment expects us to be in a set place at a set time and concentrate on a set job. The chaos tends to be predictable, even for those in erratically crisis-prone jobs, like firefighters or budget directors.

At home, especially with a family around us, anything can happen and all of it's our responsibility. The ceiling falls into the bathtub, the gerbil bites the baby, the baby drinks the Windex, the pipes freeze, there's a bat in the bedroom or a dead mouse in the oven or a burglar in the living room, the bank threatens to foreclose on the mortgage, and we're expected to cope. At work, most of us can pass the buck, or some of the bucks. Even the CEO can hand it to the board of directors, who can hand it to the stockholders.

On the job, we know what we're supposed to be doing at any given moment. At home we rarely do, and if we did, there's still no way to organize the priorities. Even while we're gathering up the trash the dog spread over the kitchen floor, we wonder if we ought to be paying bills instead, while at that very moment the children have found a ladder and are preparing to maroon the baby on the roof. Usually, at work, someone has set limits on what can happen; in the anarchy of home, the worst-case scenario changes hourly.

Besides, work often supplies us with jobs that need to be done only once. This seldom happens at home, where most work is cyclical rather than linear and needs to be repeated — the same dishes into the same dishwasher — several hundred times a year. There is no glow of accomplishment, no satisfying farewell click of finished job and forward step to new one. Home is a muddle, even for bachelors, as they rummage for the other sock and wonder whether the cat is merely coughing or about to vomit.

So, out of the limitless, unpredictable chaos of home to the limited, predictable chaos of work. We walk in and our identities fold warmly around us: we are Miss Jones the Bookkeeper, and nothing extrafiscal will be asked of us; Bob the New Accounts Man, and our only duty is to open new accounts.

If we have a desk, the chances are it will look — unlike the homebound desk — much the way we left it. We punch the computer on and it gulps and peeps its usual welcome; sharpen pencils, sniffing the fresh, schoolday smell; check our phone messages and lists of calls, our appointments book; tackle a stack of folders. All is in order. We are where we ought to be, doing what we ought to be doing. Home is far away, possibly on fire but mercifully out of our hands. Until five, our very lives, our intractable, sometimes incomprehensible lives, are out of our hands.

We're supposed to pay attention to what we're doing. There are times — if we've just fallen in love, for instance — when we'd rather think about our private lives, but more often it's a pleasure to ignore them, and because we're at work this isn't irresponsible: we're *required* to ignore them. Few are willing to admit it, but this is a major workplace benefit and the reason so many people slog through blizzards to the glad oblivion of the office.

Along with our troubles, we've left our essential confusion and helplessness behind. Here we feel useful, needed, important, grown-up. We must be, else why would they pay us? This is worth a quiet glow.

A colleague rushes in panicked; his computer has swallowed some desperately needed documents. We happen to have copies of these, correctly filed, and in a twinkling we retrieve them and hand them to him, and receive his sweaty, frantic thanks with a gracious nod. We have impressed him, earned his gratitude, and proved ourself infinitely his superior in competence. This is fun, and makes up for having to get out of bed in the morning.

Sometimes, at work, we do something extraordinarily successful, and get rewarded for it with a fond letter from the president, a promotion, a raise. This never happens at home. No matter how successful we are around the house, nobody ever gives us a raise.

Being at work justifies the day. We needn't curse ourselves for wasted hours, even if we spent them all in pointless meetings or, in a slow season, frittered them away with gossip, the newspapers, and computer games. After all, we were there; we were paid for our time. For those at home — freelances, consultants, poets, painters, pieceworkers, housewives — having done nothing all day produces hand-wringing guilt and anxiety, but for us, actual accomplishment is rather beside the point. We can walk out at five with our heads held high: another day, another dollar.

If we make a mess in the office, throw papers on the floor, leave our lunch remains lying about, very likely someone else is paid to clean up after us. For women and bachelors, this is sheer, childish glee: crumple the page, toss it over the shoulder; we're too important here to waste our valuable time on trash.

Familiar faces surround us. Our colleagues, friend and foe, are the heart of what we'll miss when unemployed. Office contacts have a flavor all their own. Office friends take less maintenance than purely social ones; you needn't make an effort to get together with them, and you aren't expected to clean up your apartment or cook dinner for them. They are always underfoot, like family, at least until they quit or get fired. You always have something to talk about with them; you needn't search for conversational gambits. And they have limits. Office friends rarely weep on your shoulder, make you responsible for their private burdens, or borrow your lawn mower. Your spouse can't take an implacable dislike to them and quarrel with their politics; neither is he or she likely to lure them into bed, causing strife. You can have lunch with them, taking pleasure in your shared concerns, and at five put them away in a desk drawer.

Even office foes have their advantages. Like office chaos, they have limits, and aren't going to poison your dog or punch you in the eye at a sales meeting. An office feud is more chess game than brawl, and played according to certain mean but unbreakable rules. Sometimes you even win, and taste the soaring joy of watching the enemy clean out his or her desk, en route to the branch office in Redfield, South Dakota. Not all pleasures are kindly ones.

In recent years the shadow of corporate downsizing has fallen over our workday comforts, and many of us once paid by the week are now paid by the hour, or by the job, or not at all. The unfamiliar faces of temps and part-timers rattle our Monday mornings, and Miss Jones the Bookkeeper has been replaced by a bookkeeping service made up of migrant workers who drift from office to office as the need arises, like fruit-pickers following ripe fruit.

And some who were once daily colleagues have been sent home as "independent contractors," with the privileges of telecommuting and buying their own health insurance.

Sometimes they come to the office anyway and hang around, wistfully, with no place to sit. Home is all very well, but home is not enough. We need the Second Place, out in the world. This is why such multitudes of women have added immeasurably to their burdens by taking outside jobs that are often, or maybe usually, even duller and less challenging than home. They're *not* home. That's the point.

Work, being largely an artificial concept now that we've all quit farming, protects us from real life. Those of us who have no work to go to get our noses rubbed in real life all day.

Not Working

FOR various reasons, some of us don't go off to work in the morning.

We may be so indecently rich as to make employment unnecessary, and all the world's pleasures are ours for the asking. We may be telecommuters. We may be retired, sent home from our jobs to putter around in the basement making birdhouses from a kit.

We may have been fired, laid off, RIFfed (fancy talk meaning reduction in force, now used as a verb) or MIAed (management-initiated attrition, ditto). In that case we're worried about money and expected to spend the whole day making phone calls begging casual acquaintances for a job. This is called networking, and it's hardly any fun at all, especially if we have only four or five possible contacts and call each of them several times a day until they foam at the mouth and rip their phones out of the wall.

Or we may have work that we do at home instead of in an office, and spend every spring trying to persuade the Internal Revenue Service that our dining-room table is really a desk.

Or we may be mothers, or even fathers, kept home by small children; this is sometimes fun and sometimes deadly.

Or we may be only temporarily and unexpectedly unemployed, like the snow-belt mother faced with a snow day. This involves a radio on the breakfast table reeling off the code numbers of schools to be closed (it's not necessary to write down your school's number; the children learned it in September). When it's official that there will indeed be no school, she calls her office and takes off her working shoes and puts her bedroom slippers back on. This day is a gift. Only the hyperactive would chain the kids to the television set so they can clean out the hall closet. It's a day to sit on the floor and play Monopoly with them; to send them out to throw snowballs and greet them home again with hot cocoa; to go sledding, sing, and read stories. A mother day, to pay off past neglects and bank against future business trips. Probably all hell is breaking loose at the office, but nothing can be done about it. The schools are closed; all bets are off.

Playing mommy on a snow day is a rare pleasure, brightened by the certainty that tomorrow the roads will be cleared, the school bus will function, and mommy will be back in the office where she belongs, a grown-up again.

What joy we find in not working depends heavily on circumstances and temperament, but clothing — or the lack thereof — always counts in freedom's favor. I have a freelancing friend who, in the summer, wears nothing at all while working, but some people find it hard to take anything seriously in the nude and besides, the chair sticks to the flesh.

For optimum mental health, *some* daytime clothing is recommended. Spending a day in pajamas can feel deliciously indolent; spending a month in them gets depressing. We feel unnecessary, since whoever heard of being necessary in pajamas? In sneakers, jeans, sweatsuits, or shorts we can still gloat merrily over the employed: "Isn't he roasting in that suit?"; "Isn't she freezing in that skirt? And look at those shoes — the agony!" We dress for luxurious ease, and go barefoot in summer.

Some advisors say job seekers should put on business clothes every morning, even without a prospective interview or any errand more formal than the supermarket, because a suit makes us feel important and businesslike, and defends the ego against the assaults of rejection. This is nonsense. The ego that depends on dry goods for its nourishment is not worth feeding, and besides, daily-worn clothes need cleaning more often, and cleaning costs money. And what if someone calls us in for an unexpected interview and there's the good suit all covered with grass stains because we were mowing the lawn in it? No, no, leave the suit neatly in the closet;

there will be plenty of time to change. Suitlessness is one of the rewards of unemployment; only an ingrate would reject the privilege.

Another dependable pleasure is the morning traffic report. In congested areas it's broadcast every ten minutes or so, and we can relish it all from our breakfast table; traffic jam on our toast, so to speak. We can even listen to it on the clock radio by the bed, snuggling the blankets under our chin and savoring reports on the fog, the icy roads, the malfunctioning traffic lights.

In really rotten weather, our local television station will send a crew out for the evening rush hour, and we can make ourself a drink, curl our toes more deeply into our bedroom slippers, and watch the unending lines of traffic, slush under their creeping tires, snow whirling in their headlights.

Here is one of the basic, atavistic pleasures left from the Early Stone Age and now almost extinct: obeying the weather's suggestions. The employed must needs go out when no sane person would, and then stay inside when the heavens smile. On a balmy summer day, the jobless can take the newspaper to the park and read the Help Wanteds on a sunny bench; in a sleet storm we needn't even get out of bed. The weather speaks, and we answer. Go for a walk in the woods or browse in a bookstore all afternoon. Play golf, go to the zoo or a matinee, or sit on the couch in our underwear eating candy bars and watching television game shows. Read the Hundred Greatest Books of the Western World. Drink beer for breakfast. Dig in the garden. Breed Pekingese. Sleep till noon.

For the jobless with a taste for anarchy, each day drops into the hands like a lump of clay to be shaped at will. Each morning is pure possibility, like a newly fertilized egg.

Some of us find in ourselves such a talent for joblessness that we quickly become unemployable and end up eking out a living peddling Coke bottles and broken toasters at flea markets. Others, desperate for the structured life, go mad with confusion and boredom, and scramble to trade in the joys of freedom for any sort of job at all. They'd rather bag groceries at the Kashway; they'd rather commute half the night. They'd rather be galley slaves.

It's a question of temperament.

Bare Feet

TWO out of every five adults take off their shoes whenever they can, and the other three don't seem to mind having their feet smothered.

I arrive at this figure by way of my own family. One of my brothers and I go barefoot even in winter, to the continuing echo of our mother's voice saying, "Aren't your feet cold?" and "Where are your shoes?" and "Put something on your *feet!*" Our three siblings wear shoes. Or sandals, or bedroom slippers, or sometimes just socks, but always something to render their feet deaf and blind. I don't know whether or not there's a genetic component involved.

My brother and I don't long to rip off the rest of our clothes; we don't wear impractical shoes; our feet in shoes don't hurt; we aren't seeking relief from the pinch. It's just that we're always, at some level of consciousness, aware of whatever's wrapped around us down there, as of a hand lightly but immovably across our mouths all day. For us and others like us, the moment of taking off the footwear is a relief and a joy, and in summer, with the barefoot hours extended into days, our personalities change. Barefoot, we're almost always at peace. We're gentle and tolerant with our fellow man. Stress and anxiety evaporate and grief itself seems bearable as long as our feet are free.

The therapeutic technique called, for some reason, "reflexology" and held by its practitioners to be an ancient healing art, is based on the massage of the feet and hands. Rub the sole and instep properly, bend the right toes, and pain and tension fall away from the whole person. Some of us can get the same effect just by slipping off the loafers. For some of us, the soul is resident in the sole, and yearns ceaselessly for light and air and self-expression. Our feet are our very selves. The touch of floor or carpet, grass or mud or asphalt, speaks to us loud and clear from the foot, that scorned and lowly organ as dear to us as our eyes and ears.

I read an interview with a very old and famous woman who was asked what she'd do differently in life if she had it to do over. After some thought, she replied that she'd start going barefoot earlier in the season.

It may be significant that our formality, our business status, our seriousness and dressedness are all directly related to sternly fettered feet. Only the lowliest employees wear sneakers or boat shoes; only the least of social occasions allow a woman to wear low heels, and only nurses can wear them to work. The only comfortable modern shoes are worn not for comfort but for strenuous, often painful, exercising. Bare feet are acceptable nowhere but on beaches, where we can't be expected to accomplish anything anyway.

Maybe the whole world secretly understands that free feet produce a different, more philosophical, relaxed, and unbusinesslike mindset. Without shoes, our ambitions would fade away, wolfish trade practices seem too much trouble, international frictions look foolish. Armies would curl up to take a nap. Nobody would get any serious work done and the world would go straight to hell.

Considered in this light, going barefoot is almost as much a vice as a pleasure. Subversive. Counterproductive, like smoking pot. Which isn't likely to stop us two out of five who revel in it.

Yes, Mother, some of the time our feet *are* cold. And yes, we do run the risk of stepping on bits of broken glass in the house and, outside, bees in the clover. As they say in the Pentagon, it's an acceptable risk. Highly acceptable.

Lunch

L UNCH is, or ought to be, time-out. A breather; a clearing halfway across the jungle of the day. Alas, it's often mere necessity, purely utilitarian nourishment to get us through till dinner — a peanut-butter sandwich at the kitchen table with a two-year-old; salad in a plastic container at the desk, dribbling ranch dressing on the keyboard. But when we can thrust the day apart in the middle and meet someone in a restaurant for lunch, it's pleasure. Dinner tends to be an integral part of the social or family fabric; lunch is our own. Lunch is an island; lunch is insulated front and back from the halves of the workday.

Even a business lunch is more amiable than the business that surrounds it. Manners improve. The tablecloth serves as a flag of truce, and sections of the conversation are reserved, however awkwardly, for topics of general interest. Only second-degree, or noncontentious, business is conducted; preliminary sparring, background material, summaries, feelers. Lunch, with its confidential privacy, may be step three in the job-interview process, far from the ears of your present employer, but actual contracts are rarely signed among the plates and glasses, and serious bargaining takes place before or after, in the office, where it belongs.

In more reckless and carefree days, the restaurant lunch called for a preliminary drink. This was a kind of badge or seal of its specialness, the paper party-hat it wore, since who shakes up a martini before lunching on a ham-and-cheese at the desk?

Drinks were once obligatory for out-of-town clients. They came in from Altoona as if shot from a cannon, to see the new line or the new campaign or sign the new contract, and expected to kick up their heels, released from the supervisions of home. This was lovely for the away team, every few weeks or months, but it took its toll on the home team, who sometimes drank through five of such celebrations in a work-week. It cut seriously into afternoon productivity. Three o'clock in the afternoon is a metabolic low point anyway, and martini lunches encourage naps. Nowadays many firms insist on bottled water for the hosts, and many visitors are shamed into abstinence beside them. It's a pity, since water, even French or Italian water, is only water, never a paper party-hat.

Another joy of the business lunch is that either someone else is paying for it or you plan to deduct it: the host who picks up the check enjoys the sensation of control and condescension; the guest enjoys free food.

The purely social lunch rejoices in a seclusion rarely found at other meals. We're away from our homes, our offices, our families, and the obligations of the morning and afternoon. Probably no one in the restaurant knows, or cares, who we are or whom we're with. We can lunch with people we wouldn't otherwise see, people too far outside our normal circles or people we've been forbidden to know. We can lunch, tentatively, with long-estranged relatives. No one can dine tentatively; dinner represents commitment.

Traditionally, lunch is the hour when women meet, cementing their friendship with confidences that rarely flow during the more public, formal, and often mixed-sex dinner hour. It's a secret section of time uniquely our own, heralded by the small frisson of pleasure as we walk into the restaurant, as carefree and independent as most of us get to be in an average day.

Dinner is an obligatory meal. Lunch, and lunch partners, we can choose, often on the spur of the moment, and cancel if we want to, even at the last minute, pleading business.

Lunch with lovers, past, present, or possible, enjoys an anarchy, a severing of our connections to life's duties, rather like the sea voyages of former days, when self-limiting flirtations flourished and responsibility dropped from one's shoulders. Romantically, because of its time brackets, lunch is a tease, a question mark, a dropped handkerchief. (Such heedless afternoons as the one in Cézanne's *Déjeuners sur l'herbe* don't count; that was France.)

We can safely lunch with a stranger whose attractions we're unsure of, because dinner is open-ended and the whole shapeless mass of the night lies beyond it, but after lunch we'll part for our separate workplaces, maybe never to meet again. Lunch can even be artificially limited; we can glance at our watch and remember a meeting or the school bus.

The restaurant lunch may be a purer pleasure than the restaurant dinner. Dinner is part of the larger evening; lunch is self-contained, an interlude, a frivolous jewel glowing in the trash-pile of the day. Besides, we can tell ourselves we deserve it. If we've spent the morning either working or looking for work or surrounded by fractious toddlers, lunch, preferably with friend or lover, is a reward, in a way that breakfast and dinner never are. We can lunch smugly.

Buying Things

S HOPPING is considered America's second-favorite leisure pastime, next only after television, but shopping is different from buying things. Shopping's popularity seems to have grown with the malls, which some people hate and others can't stay away from.

Malls are recent. First there was a shopping street or block lined with stores, most of which had display windows. Walking up and down admiring the goods set forth in these was called "window shopping," and was practiced only on foot and only in fair weather. Then cars proliferated and gave birth to the shopping center. This was a cluster of stores centered around free off-street parking, but each store was still a distinct entity and you still got wet going from one to another in the rain.

Then, somewhere around 1970, came the mall, and the mall was a *place*, like a small climate-controlled city with merchandise as its citizenry, and the stores were reduced to elements of a larger whole, like the peas in pea soup. It was a grand idea and caught hold right away, not because we needed to buy things but because we'd been longing for a place to go to get out of the house. A dry, warmed or cooled place with free admission, full of faces and movement. People who live in actual cities, once the natural habitat of stores, drive out to the suburban malls, and people in rural areas and small towns, frantic with boredom at home, practically live in them. A long Saturday afternoon can be spent ambling around and around, licking an ice-cream cone or nibbling a doughnut, drifting in and out of dozens or hundreds of shops without noticing their names. Teenagers arrange to meet there and drift around in groups. Probably there's a theater showing several movies at once. By the end of the day surprisingly few people are carrying packages; buying things wasn't the point.

Indeed, for some of us, buying things there is almost impossible. Some of us always feel hopelessly lost in malls, and threatened by the pressure of so much merchandise on all sides. Individual character blurs; no dress surrounded by half a million dresses can have the panache of the single gown in a Main Street shop window. Sometimes it all runs together, and sneakers become indistinguishable from cosmetics, skis from stereo sets, books from bed linens. We panic and rush for the exit, but it's the wrong exit, and we may never find our car again, let alone the sneakers we came to buy.

Others, I hear, are stimulated by the sight of consumer goods in bulk, and buy reckless armfuls of things they don't particularly want and have no use for, running themselves deeply into debt.

For better or worse, malls are here to stay because they fill a basic social need, but it's a different need from buying things. There may even be a difference between "things" and merchandise, the latter being produced solely to be sold and the former existing for reasons of their own. It's these that we should snatch to our bosoms when they speak to us, whether we can afford them or not.

I don't mean mass-produced goods that folks are going to go on urging us to buy for the rest of our lives; obviously if we can't afford the new car or the CD player this year we can buy an improved version of it next year or the year after. But life is full of one-time offers which, like love, we should seize on the spot or we'll be sorry.

I keep struggling with an unfortunate Puritan tendency to self-denial, and sometimes it sabotages me. There was that quilt of appliquéd tulips at the county fair, for instance. It wasn't expensive, really, not considering the hours of patient, blinding work that went into its making, but I wrestled with my conscience and lost; I didn't really need it. I thought about it for years, though, and finally went out and bought a different quilt. It was far more expensive and not nearly so pretty, but I needed it to expunge the loss of the tulips.

At least you can sleep under a quilt. Sometimes it's the totally useless, the most arrant, inexcusable luxury that stretches out its hands and begs to be ours. There was the red bird in the cage, still haunting me ten years later.

The stylish little gift shop in my town was going out of business, to general regret, and everything was half price. Including the red bird. It was as bright and cleverly wrought as any real bird that ever perched, and it lived in an elegant golden hanging cage. When you wound the key it bowed to left and right and sang a birdsong of such piercing, complicated sweetness it brought tears to the eyes.

Even at half price it was expensive. I walked away birdless. The moment of relinquishment is still clear in my mind, like that moment at the airport when you blew a kiss to the lover you'd never see again, though you didn't know that at the time.

If I'd bought the bird, I would have been pressed for money for a while. It would have made a hole in the bank account, but by now the hole would be long mended; I'm no richer today for leaving the bird behind. And if I'd taken it home, by now it would have been singing to me for years and years of dark and foggy days.

I don't always lose. Once, during one of my deepest plunges into poverty, I bought a pair of bath towels. I'd been poor for so long that everything I owned had gone shabby and ratty-looking; all my possessions seemed scummed over by a gray film of meanness and want. My towels were thin and scratchy and I kept clipping the loose strings from their edges. In a burst of defiance I went out and bought a pair of scarlet bath towels of the very finest quality, soft and dense and thick as cream. It was a great blow to the budget and I ate bread and cheese for a week, but for years the towels cheered me every morning of my life. I felt less poor, and by and by I was less poor.

Owning things is lovely. Not merchandise other people want us to buy, not equipment we think we should have because others do, but the things that some higher destiny has earmarked for our own. When the red bird sings to you, *buy it.*

Saving Money

THIS is a pleasure comparable to smoking cigarettes, in that it can be highly addictive, hazardous to the health, and a pain to your friends and relations.

Most of us can take it or leave it. We may stock up on what's cheap at the supermarket, we may wait for the sales before buying a suit, but nothing prevents us from latching on to some really decent champagne when the occasion warrants. Some, on the other hand, are genetically susceptible to obsession.

These unfortunates come to believe that a penny saved is truly a penny earned, instead of a nuisance that weights down your pockets. Perhaps they begin moderately enough, switching long-distance phone companies back and forth for the introductory rates, cheating on their taxes, and saving twenty dollars on a plane ticket that takes them to Houston by way of Banff. Most of us, as I said, can stop there, or any time we want to, and there's much to be said for a good thrift shop and the heady feeling of walking into it knowing we can afford anything, even everything, in the whole store, though this leads to overcrowded closets. But the addicts develop an odd, mad glitter in their eye at the thought of having beaten the system. They roll up their sleeves and prowl the budget for fresh savings.

Their hearts beat high as they turn the thermostat down to sixty and hide all but one of the lightbulbs. Intoxicated, they shop for last week's bread, last month's vegetables, and shapeless garments for a dime from the Salvation Army. A penny spent is a penny mourned, even if it's someone else's; take them out to dinner and the *truite meunière* is ashes in their mouth at the thought of all that cheaper food back home. They cancel the newspaper; plenty of perfectly good papers left on the commuter train. Carrying false identification, they queue up for government-issue cheese. At Christmas they give everyone cookies made from flour-and-water paste, and when their children go out in public, strangers offer them spare change.

I'm not sneering at the pleasure of it. Pleasure is good, and I have watched loved ones in the grip of this addiction and I can't deny their happiness, but this is a dangerous joy. These are the people the police find starved and frozen in furnished rooms with a million dollars in the bank.

Probably not more than one in ten carries the gene for this delirious parsimony, but it's wise not to take the chance.

Buy at retail, use hundred-watt bulbs, and leave the thermostat at seventy.

Naps

IN France, on a rented canal boat, my friends and I gazed in despair at the closed oaken gates of the lock. We'd come to them only seconds after the witching hour of noon, but we were too late. There was no one to open the lock for us; *l'éclusière* was at lunch, and after lunch she would lay herself down, close her eyes, and nap. At two, but not before, she would emerge refreshed from her square granite house and set the great cogs in motion.

We tied the boat up to a spindly bush beside the towpath and waited. And waited. It was high haying season, but the fields lay empty of farmers. The roads lay empty of trucks. France lunched, and then slept. So did Spain. So did much of the civilized world.

If we'd been differently nurtured we too would have taken a nap, but we were Americans, condemned from the age of four to trudge through our sleepless days. Americans are afraid of naps.

Napping is too luxurious, too sybaritic, too unproductive, and it's free; pleasures for which we don't pay make us anxious. Besides, it seems to be a natural inclination. Those who get paid to investigate such things have proved that people deprived of daylight and their wristwatches, with no notion of whether it was night or day, sink blissfully asleep in midafternoon as regular as clocks. Fighting off natural inclinations is a major Puritan virtue, and nothing that feels that good can be respectable.

They may have a point there. Certainly the process of falling asleep in the afternoon is quite different from bedtime sleep.

Whether this is physiological or merely a by-product of guilt, it's a blatantly sensual experience, a voluptuous surrender, akin to the euphoric swoon of the heroine in a vampire movie. For the self-controlled, it's frightening — *how far down am I falling? will I ever climb back?* The sleep itself has a different texture. It's blacker, thicker, more intense, and works faster. Fifteen minutes later the napper pops back to the surface as from time travel, bewildered to find that it's only ten of two instead of centuries later.

Like skydiving, napping takes practice; the first few tries are scary.

The American nap is even scarier because it's unilateral. Sleeping Frenchmen are surrounded by sleeping compatriots, but Americans who lie down by day stiffen with the thought of the busy world rushing past. There we lie, visible and vulnerable on our daylit bed, ready to cut the strings and sink into the dark, swirling, almost sexual currents of the impending doze, but what will happen in our absence? Our stocks will fall; our employees will mutiny and seize the helm; our clients will tiptoe away to competitors. Even the housewife, taking advantage of the afternoon lull, knows at the deepest level of consciousness that the phone is about to ring.

And of course, for those of us with proper jobs, there's the problem of finding a bed. Some corporations, in their concern for their employees' health and fitness, provide gym rooms where we can commit strenuous exercise at lunchtime, but where are our beds? In Japan, the productivity wonder of the industrialized world, properly run companies maintain a nap room wherein the workers may refresh themselves. Even in America, rumor has it, the costly CEOs of giant corporations work sequestered in private suites, guarded by watchpersons, mainly so they can curl up unseen to sharpen their predatory powers with a quick snooze. A couple of recent presidents famous for their all-night energies kept up the pace by means of naps. Other presidents, less famous for energy, slept by day *and* night; woe to the unwary footstep that wakened Coolidge in the afternoon.

This leaves the rest of us lackeys bolt upright, toughing it out, trying to focus on the computer screen, from time to time snatching our chins up off our collarbones and glancing furtively around to see if we were noticed. The modern office isn't designed for privacy, and most of our cubicles have no doors to close, only gaps in the portable partitions. Lay our heads down on the desk at the appropriate hour and we're exposed to any passing snitch who strolls the halls enforcing alertness. It's a wonder they don't walk around ringing bells and blowing trumpets from one till three. American employers do not see the afternoon forty winks as refreshing the creative wellsprings of mere employees. They see it as goofing off.

Apparently most of us agree. Large numbers of us are, for one reason or another, home-bound, but do we indulge in the restorative nap? Mostly not. Even with no witness but ourselves, we're ashamed to. It would mean we weren't busy. We tell ourselves we have a million urgent things to do and our lives are so full and exciting we couldn't possibly lie down by daylight. Never mind that our heads are no particular use in midafternoon and half the work we do may need to be redone in the cold light of tomorrow morning. Oozing virtue and busyness, we flog ourselves on till evening.

In the evening, at least according to the cartoons, American men fall asleep on the couch, after dinner, a-flicker with light from the television screen. They are home from work, the day's toil accomplished, and they're free to doze, though if they'd napped at the biologically appointed time they wouldn't need to now, and at this hour it's not so much a nap as an awkward preview of the night's sleep, possibly leading to four-a.m. insomnia. Women, on the other hand, are never home from work unless it's someone else's home; home for them is simply different work, and naps are not an option.

It's time to rethink the nap from both the corporate and the personal viewpoint.

Those CEOs who find their own naps such an asset to productivity might consider what they'd do for the rest of us. They could hire consultants to conduct productivity studies, dividing us into teams of sleepers and wakers. When the results were in, they might even decide to mandate naps, as naps were mandated in nursery school, when we each unfolded a name-tagged blanket and spread it on the floor and lay down and shut up for a while. Granted we can't all have office suites, or even couches, and it would be unseemly to have us stacked up like firewood on the conference table, but we could use futons, stored discreetly under the desk, or folding cots, or sleeping bags. The phones could be left to their answering devices, the faxes could pile up in the hopper, and the sales reps could pound in vain on the door as they'd find themselves doing in France.

Those of us at home, with beds at hand, should take pleasure as well as productivity into account. Consider the cat. A perfectly healthy cat can nap through the entire month of February and wake feeling all the better for it. The house may be simply pattering with uncaught mice, but no twitch of guilt quivers the whiskers of the napping cat. In summer he stretches out to full length, preferably in a breezy doorway where he's rather in the way, and sometimes on his back, looking dead enough to alarm the chance visitor, and drapes his arm over his eyes. Swiftly and easily he lowers himself into sleep, sensuous, fur-lined sleep, the sleep of the untroubled conscience. Nothing tells him he ought to be rushing about his various occupations. Sleep, for a cat, is a worthy occupation in itself.

Let us consider the cat and go to bed. Bed the haven, the motherly lap, the downy nest. Bed, from which Earth with its fuss and fidgeting shrinks to the size of Pluto, visible only by telescope. We should loosen or remove some of our clothing, close the curtains, and lie down flat, allowing the vital forces to circulate through the brain and restore its muscle tone.

Bed is *not* a shameful, shiftless place to be by day, nor is it necessary to run a fever of 102 to deserve it. Bed can even be productive. The effortless horizontal body and the sensory deprivation of the quiet bedroom leave the mind free, even in sleep, to focus, to roam, sometimes to forge ahead. Knotty problems can unknot themselves as if by magic. Creative solutions can tiptoe across the coverlet and nestle onto the pillow of the napper, even while the black velvet paws of Morpheus lie closely over his eyes. He may wake half an hour later with the road ahead laid clear.

Creativity doesn't come a-running to those who toil and slave for her; she's as much the daughter of rest and play as of effort. Just because we're uncomfortable doesn't mean we're productive; just because we're comfortable doesn't mean we're lazy. Milton wrote

Paradise Lost in bed. Winston Churchill, a prodigious producer, wrote all those large important histories in bed, brandy bottle at the ready. No doubt when inspiration flagged and his thoughts refused to marshal, he took a nip and a nap. Now, there was a man who knew a thing or two about a good day's work.

Happy Hour

I N the olden days, the returning breadwinner was greeted by his wife at the door with a perfectly chilled martini; sometimes, at least in cartoons, she positively rushed down the front walk with it. It restored his soul, loosened his tightly coiled nerves, and punctuated the day, closing off the business portion and ushering in the evening.

After a few happy decades of this, she went out and got a job, and he was greeted at the door by a basket of dirty laundry instead. It's just not the same.

Breadwinners of both sexes are still free, however, to stop off in a bar. Except in the most sophisticated areas, bars in America have long been considered slightly shady. We look at them, not as relaxed and sociable watering holes, therapeutic respites from business and domestic cares, but as haunts of shabby sin. Hangouts for the desperately unhappy and predatory persons of all genders. Hideouts for the irresponsible, with discreet curtains across their storefront windows to conceal the denizens from prying neighbors; where the ringing phone is greeted with "If it's my wife, I'm not here."

We aren't supposed to be drinking after work anyway, we're supposed to be exercising or picking the kids up from day care.

This is a shame, as a good bar is a great joy in life and a fine place to be after the day's work.

Recent studies have shown that red wine, even quite large quantities of red wine, helps prevent heart disease, and this comes as good news to those who would rather stop off in a bar than a gym. We can use it as a wedge. We can stop off at the neighborhood tappy with the same self-satisfied expression we used to wear jogging, pound on the mahogany, and demand a glass of the house red. Once our consciences have adjusted to the new regime, we can order a Boodles martini, straight up, and pretend it's red.

For the perfect happy hour, it should be summer, blistering hot, the streets clogged with ill-tempered rush-hour traffic and the melting asphalt soft underfoot. Our workday should have been frantic but ultimately successful. After the glare outside, the bar should be almost pitch dark, icily air conditioned, and smell of black leather banquettes, and we should be meeting someone there. If we're male, she ought to wear a short skirt and have silky knees, jauntily crossed as she turns to greet us from the bar stool. If we're female, he ought to be glancing anxiously over his shoulder for us, and light up incandescently with pleasure and relief when we come in.

Then, knees touching, neck muscles relaxing, brow drying in the cold dry air, we should drink. Certain things were put upon this earth for our enjoyment, and it's wasteful and wicked to contemn them.

Mail

NOT all mail is a pleasure, but the *fact* of mail is nice. Even today it has an aura about it, like something fetched by Mercury, messenger to the gods of Olympus; we know he wouldn't bring phone calls or faxes, but he might bring letters — mail goes back as far as the written word and still bulges with mythic possibilities.

Of course, ninety percent of it is inexplicable. Someone somewhere has written, photographed, and printed it; someone else carried it to us and stuffed it in the box or poked it through the slot. We unpack it or gather it up from the floor and dump it in the trash, which later we put out for still other people to pick up and drive to a landfill. That's its life cycle, and it would seem futile even to an aphid. At least aphids reproduce.

Most of the rest is bills or the bad news somebody couldn't face telling us over the phone. We know this, but just the same we rummage through it all, always hoping for something worthily Mercurian. A contract, a letter, a postcard. A message from a stranger that opens up whole new landscapes. Love. Money.

Those devoted to technological progress keep trying to convince us that mail is obsolete, that we don't need it in these perfected times, and any day now even the bills will be mysteriously communicated to our bank, which will mysteriously, if we have enough on deposit, pay them whether we like it or not. Personal messages will appear via E-mail on our computers. Then, they say, there'll be nothing left but the junk, and that can come in by fax instead.

They're wrong. We'll hang on to mail because it's one of life's small recurring pleasures. It arrives daily at its appointed hour — unlike the bullying phone that rings when it pleases — to await our convenience. A mailless holiday has a dead spot at its center. He who says "I don't know, I haven't look at my mail in a week" has abandoned all hope of change or drama or romance and slipped into clinical depression. The mail's our daily dose of promise.

Mixed in with the other junk are catalogs of books, clothes, and gadgets that just might contain the single perfect item that will change our lives forever. There are sweepstakes we just might win. Magazines, and no matter what toppling piles of unread magazines already encumber our floor, the new ones look, briefly, as if they had something important to tell us; after all, they came to us personally, with our name on them, unlike radio and television that blather indiscreetly to all.

I'm on the lists of dozens of travel enterprises and my mailbox is wedged with luminescent invitations from the world. Schooners in the Caribbean, barges on the Nile, vaporettos on the Grand Canal. Tented safaris in Kenya, archaeological digs in Turkey, and now a whole new geography of ancient cities released from Russia's ex-empire. The Andes, the Alps, the Himalayas; the Rhone, the Rhine, the Seine. I read them, and just for a moment I imagine that maybe, somehow, this time, I'll go. It's a nice moment. On moonier days I save them, because you never know — tomorrow's mail may bring the $10,000 check for the trip to Egypt.

Once in a while, we even get a letter. Contrary to popular belief, some people still write letters, though maybe not the long, witty, chatty, literate, two-way correspondences of yore that, bound in hardcover, make such fine bedtime reading. We still write because in a letter we can say what we mean to say, instead of blurting something clumsily into the phone, forgetting what we really meant to say and then, later, forgetting what it was we did say. We write because the recipient can read and reread it at leisure, at the comfortable time, over a cup of tea, instead of being forced to listen on the phone, dripping in a towel or halfway through dinner or halfway out the door. If there are questions, the answers can be pondered. And a letter, unlike the evanescent phone call or the electronic E-mail, is physical, and we can save it for the record or for sentiment's sake. And it's private; reading other people's mail is a recognized sin far blacker than listening to their phone calls or logging on to their electronic devices.

For all the above reasons, there are still love letters. (I understand that love tape-recordings are newly popular among the semi-literate, but they too come by mail.) Love letters, as always, can be bundled and tied in ribbon and kept in the attic, so our grandchildren can read them on a rainy day and shriek with laughter that anyone ever felt that way about dreary old us.

Whatever our past disappointments in it, today's bundle of mail from Mercury's hand still feels more promising than the ringing phone from Mr. Bell's. Maybe we can't even name the message we expect, but we feel in our bones that when it does come, this is the way it will come, because this is how the gods get in touch.

Therefore, even if nobody's likely to write us a love letter, we come home every day and look at the mail. You never know.

Dinner

DINNER has fallen on sad days. Forty years ago, many quite ordinary people had their dinner cooked for them by hired help, who were often pretty good at the job and understood such esoteric matters as dumplings rising fatly on the simmering chicken pieces, nestled among bits of aromatic celery and smelling of rosemary.

Failing this, dinner was cooked by the lady of the house, who had varying degrees of talent but at least accepted what was expected.

It was a lot of work. Looking back on our childhood, many of us remember the fruits of this labor. Mashed potatoes made of real potatoes, with a dent in the middle to hold the thick, dark gravy. Freshly shelled peas, popping between the teeth to release the very essence of spring gardens. Onion soup, with its glowing, complex, oniony, long-simmered broth and gooey strands of cheese. The warm nutmeg-and-cinnamon breath of an apple pie. Tiny spicy meatballs in a savory sauce. The rumpled, swollen soufflé, pregnant with airy bliss, yearning to be violated.

Hard work, all of it.

Children came home from school and headed to the kitchen for a cookie, to be shooed back out again by a woman making dinner. Stirring, tasting, measuring, beating, slicing. Shucking corn. Whipping egg whites. An hour later the house was filled with anticipatory smells of cooking. Every proper home, by six in the evening, smelled of dinner, and these scents were as much the signal of day's end as the muted rattle or hiss of curtains being drawn. The gastric juices woke, yawned, stretched deliciously, and made ready. Proper husbands, martini in hand, were expected to say, "Smells good, what is it?"

Dinner was a daily event, the shared ceremony that was almost a synonym for family life. Children were required to wash their hands in its honor and forbidden to nibble beforehand and spoil their appetites. ("Appetite" is a word we rarely hear now, but back then a hearty one was considered, as it still is in France, a sign of happiness and vigor and a necessary compliment to the cook.)

The dinner table itself was something of an icon; no quarrels were permitted in its area and disagreeable matters were not to be mentioned in its presence. An inconsiderate phone ringing at "the dinner hour" was left unanswered, or the caller brushed off sternly with "We're eating dinner." Interrupting dinner was a sin. Coming home late for it was punishable. An insult to dinner was an insult to all.

Currently the experts are urging us to gather the family like this for a meal at least once a week, but it isn't easy to arrange. All the domestic cooks, paid or unpaid, have found more interesting or profitable ways to spend their weekday afternoons. The food packagers sprang into the gap with boxed, frozen, or plastic-bagged dinners that, inexplicably, never smell of anything at all. The lady of the house, coming home late from the office, needn't panic, needn't start peeling potatoes in her good blue suit; dinner, though scentless, will be ready in a flash. With the microwave standing by, she needn't even worry about choosing a menu acceptable to all hands, since each person can eat a separate dinner, perhaps even in a separate room, at various hours, pizza for Joe, potpie for Suzy, and something Chinese, boiled in a plastic bag, for Henry. To the person responsible, this convenience is more than enjoyable, it's downright essential.

During the week, we eat our odorless food and toss its containers in the trash, but on weekends, grand dinners can be made, often featuring meat cooked on the barbecue grill by the man of the house, since outdoor cooking is more manly, more Paleolithic, than stove cooking. It even smells manly, and the mix of smoke and charred meat in the air reaches far back into our origins, kindling ancient responses of satisfaction. "Home is the hunter, / Home from the hill . . ." Throw another tree on the fire.

On weekends, there's even time — for those who remember how — to stuff a chicken and roast it till its skin crackles, and brew a sinful gravy from the residue in the pan. To open a bottle of wine. To offer happy thanks for the once ordinary pleasure of a dinner that smells like food.

Or, if there isn't time for chicken, we can slice an onion, throw it in the frying pan with some oil, maybe a clove of garlic, and cook it slowly. The promising scent of onions frying will penetrate every cranny of the house, gladdening the heart while we microwave some boxes. Later we can scrape the onions into the garbage.

A small but audible minority currently gets its dining pleasure from eating, as they put it, properly. These people thrill to the excitement of dodging improper foods, as if they were running zigzag through a minefield to a safe, cereal-strewn haven on the farther side. Every week they gleefully devour the latest bulletins on pesticides, cholesterol, sodium, PCBs, steroids, hormones, antibiotic supplements, butterfat, coliform bacteria, salmonella. For them, the joy of dining is in the restrictions, tightening almost daily, and the dazzling triumph of managing to get enough to eat anyway. Tucking into their well-scrubbed, steamed, butterless cauliflower and their pot of organic lentils, their hearts leap up in wonder at their own virtue and in contemplating the horrid fate of the rest of us, out there eating chicken gravy as if there were no tomorrow. Pleasure is where you find it.

If we're rich enough we can just go out and eat in a restaurant. Restaurants are expensive, and worth every penny. Just as in the old days of hired help or homebound housewives, someone else shops and chops, slices and stirs, and often comes up with something we probably couldn't do even if we did have the time. Something we've never even heard of, something ripe with new sensations, from Mexico or north China or Vietnam or Italy or Provence, often booby-trapped with benign-looking objects like those small, green, bean-shaped things from Thailand that blow your ears off and make you weep in public. Peanuts in the chicken, squid in the soup. It isn't comforting, like the rice-and-gravy of childhood, but it's exciting and takes us out of our context for a bit: a quick evening's trip to somewhere else.

Having someone cook for us and set the food before us is always a joy, especially for women; men sometimes feel, resentfully, that they should be getting this kind of service at home, as a matter of ordinary domestic course. For women, the abdication of our plain and obvious responsibility — to feed ourselves and anyone else in the immediate area — is heady stuff and glorifies the most ordinary restaurant: *We are about to eat that which we did nothing to prepare.* We didn't grow it. We didn't skin it or even slice it. Or even shop for it. In awful point of fact, when finished we aren't going to wash even our own plate, let alone everyone else's.

Even the plainest and dowdiest women, if you've ever noticed, look beautiful in restaurants. Small wonder.

Using People

U P until a generation or so ago, we could pay people to do things for us. Simple things we could probably have done ourselves. Carry our luggage. Cook our dinner. Put gas in our car. Mow our lawn. But these are more enlightened times; we're sensitive to other people's prideful entitlements, and the people who once carried luggage have realized their right not to carry it. So now we do everything singlehanded, and travel with no more clothes and books than we can lift and haul ourselves. Indeed, notices and public-address systems warn us that if someone does offer to carry our suitcase he will either seed it with bombs (freedom of political expression) or nip out the side door and sell it (free enterprise).

Once upon a time, no one of any standing at all carried anything. Staggering through the streets under bags and parcels, oranges rolling in my wake, I think of the lost generations of delivery boys. I think of the elite striding freely along while lesser beings trudged behind with the necessities, the golf clubs, shotguns, dead ducks, picnic hampers, purchases, whatever. It must have felt like heaven. Carrying things, especially when you aren't getting paid for it, is uncomfortable and vaguely embarrassing. Until quite recently, officers in the world's better-run armies were forbidden to appear in public carrying anything at all except a swagger stick, so as not to lower themselves in the eyes of the Other Ranks.

The delivery boys have vanished, whistling, into the mists of time. And except on Park Avenue, the doorman is now an electric eye, the elevator operator is a button, and services have replaced service — the laundry instead of the laundress, day care instead of nursemaids. Serving forty families is enterprise; serving one is shameful, and the shame falls equally on worker and workee.

Americans have always fought shy of the word "servant," preferring the democratic "hired help." We came over here, after all, to get away from all that bowing and scraping, and it's our birthright to thumb our nose at personal authority. We've always respected the coal miner, for instance, as a proud and independent laborer, while the family cook, stirring the soup and setting the table, warm, clean, and dry, was seen to be slaving in vilest servitude. Her daughters saw it that way too. Now there are no more cooks.

When the jobs we can't do for ourselves (psychiatry, tax preparation) call for heavy spending on our part and advanced degrees on theirs, hiring help is perfectly virtuous, but when they call for merely domestic skills or a strong back (snow shoveling, window washing) it's exploitative and morally wrong, and we should do it ourselves, regardless of the strength of our backs, until we're eighty. This is the price of democracy.

Still, no one can stop us from reading, wistfully, novels about the unenlightened upper classes of Europe and Asia and the British raj. Are there, perhaps, ladies' maids somewhere still, to zip us up the back and arrange our hair? Valets to brush the cat hair from our suit before we venture forth? Do watercress sandwiches still come, in a different world, when we ring for them? Or, as in the outposts of the Empire, gin slings and a boy with a fan when we clap? Are chauffeurs somewhere still nodding off at the wheel, waiting to drive us home through the fog, while we sweep through the last waltz?

We can tell ourselves that it must have been a flaming nuisance, all those extra people underfoot, waiting around to hand you your hat and gloves and open the door, but secretly we think we could get used to it. After all, in the better households, upper servants were waited on by lower servants and easily got used to it.

Let us cherish our last shreds of help before they too disappear. Let us take taxis, for instance. Taxis were always my own mother's benchmark of inexcusable self-indulgence, no matter how weary the walk, impossible the parking, evil the weather, or tardy the bus. Therefore they thrill me deliciously, even when the driver speaks no known human language and screams hideously when I try to correct his trajectory. For the length of the journey he is mine to command, at least in theory, and in service to me alone. I feel like a sultan. If he gets lost, it's inconvenient but it's not my fault. If he runs a light or crushes a pedestrian, the responsibility is his.

Shifting anything at all from our shoulders to other shoulders is far too rare a joy. For the most part, if dinner is burnt it is we who burnt it; if the spoons get stolen it is we who were asleep instead of on guard. Blame darkens our days.

Whenever we can manage and afford it, let us wriggle out from under our burdens. Too much has been expected of us. Let us go to a restaurant and leave cooking to the chefs. Let us leave the children to a sitter, the phones to a secretary, the car to a tow truck, the lawn to a neighbor's child, the dog at the vet's, the clothes at the cleaner's, our cough with the doctor, the party to a caterer, the toilet to a plumber, our wretched childhood to the therapist, our wretched hair to the hairdresser.

Probably Jeeves will never shimmer into the bedroom with our morning cup of tea, but wherever we can find a pair of helping hands, let us beg, bribe, or bully them into our service. Like the trailing arbutus or the peregrine falcon, it's a rare, frail, elusive pleasure these days, but a fine one.

Seasonal Food

MODERN food distribution is amazing. Walk into the supermarket in February, stamping snow off your boots, and be dazed by the mountains of fruit and vegetables from every month of the year. At any given moment, someone somewhere in the hemisphere is picking the green beans of July, the peaches and sweet corn of August, the apples of October, the brussels sprouts of winter, the asparagus of April, the cherries of June. (Or, if not actually picking them, at least hauling them out of warehouses.) The long-distance highways and skyways are dense with traveling food. It may not taste the same as when grown nearby, but in the supermarket, waxed and polished and brilliantly lighted, it glitters like a lunatic's dream of supernatural abundance.

Certainly our diets are the better for it, but we've lost some of the shapeliness of the year. Some of our ceremonies have lost their original meaning, some have vanished, and the cyclical majesty of the seasons has been cut down to size; we seem to have conquered time itself. Eating fresh, field-grown corn-on-the-cob in March, we might as well be on the spaceship *Enterprise* for all the contact we have with solid ground.

I realize it's petty to complain, and I apologize. I realize our rural ancestors staggered into spring on the edge of scurvy, heartily sick of the half-rotted cabbages packed in sand in the root cellar. Small wonder they ranged the woods and fields looking for early-growing weeds — plaintain, dock, dandelion — and cooked them up and ate them gladly. (Some of them even managed to eat skunk cabbage, boiled in many waters to leach out the smell.) And I realize that local vegetables have largely receded into myth, and our cities are ringed now with housing developments and industrial parks instead of truck farms. The roadside stands people used to drive to in search of fresh-picked food have mostly vanished, and when we do find one it's suspiciously far from signs of agriculture and the wares suspiciously similar to their brethren in the supermarket.

Still, I miss some of the rituals of the past, back when oysters needed an "r," bock beer needed April, and the turkey was the solitary lord and master of Thanksgiving instead of a year-round source of inexpensive low-fat protein.

When I lived in Philadelphia, years ago, the only sure sign of spring was the arrival of local shad. The shad worked its way slowly up the coastal waters and into such rivers as were still clean enough to be liquid, bearing spring on their shiny backs. Oh, shad would turn up in the markets earlier, trucked in from the Carolinas, but it was expensive and somehow inauthentic. We waited. Then the prices plunged — old-timers remembered buck shad at a nickel a pound — and spring was upon us. We invited all our friends to the great spring dinner: the first gin-and-tonic of the year, followed by shad, asparagus, and small round pink potatoes. At some point in the evening a silent tectonic grinding took place underfoot and the season changed.

Having waited was part of the ceremony. Waiting folded us into the orderly rhythms of life; just as there was a time for baseball and a time for football, there was a time when you could eat Winesaps and drink cider and a time when you couldn't.

Food and the wheel of the year are, or ought to be, intimately connected. As the seder means Passover and the candy cane Christmas, the peach should mean summer. This intensifies both fruit and season. Peach tastes like summer: summer tastes like peach. Having eaten the peach, and wiped our chins, a proportion of our flesh becomes summer too. Simple and satisfying. A winter peach is meaningless. Besides, it tastes like the poor starved thing it is, without enough sunlight or mother's milk in its days, picked green in some unimaginably foreign climate and sent off to ripen on the journey.

Our spring lamb comes from Australia at any old time of year, and lacks resonance; it's hard for us to imagine its previous life. Like a chocolate bunny in August, asparagus in October has lost an essential element, part of what made it significant. We're out of touch with our food.

Of course there are utilitarian, vulgar foods like lettuce that never had much aura and may come from wherever they please, but important events like sweet cherries should come in season, so we can sink our teeth into June. Suck its juices. I'm in favor of holding to local calendars, local rituals, whenever I can. We don't have enough ceremonies in our lives as it is and we can't afford to keep losing them.

Besides, the only way to get a decent tomato is still to grow it yourself, and eat it at its appointed time. Tomatoes aren't lettuce, they're aristocrats. They won't be bullied.

The distributors, amazing as they are, still can't quite bundle up the four seasons and truck them around the country like a load of wallboard. Sometimes seasons still travel under their own steam, carrying their own food, and it tastes more important for having been awaited.

Going Out

I T'S a great pity that so many of us have stopped going out at night, once a major joy in life and the main reason for group living, as in cities, instead of in isolated caves. Alas, now theaters and symphony orchestras and ballet companies struggle for funding and play to empty seats, their former customers huddled at home behind multiply-locked doors. Street crime has a lot to answer for on judgment day.

Going out in the evening opens up possibilities and invokes the unexpected. We leave the predictable shelter of our own roof and expose ourselves to the great *out* where anything can happen. We may get mugged; we may find our true love. Our car may get dinged in the parking lot. Someone may invite us to Paris, or to star in his next play. Going out, even to a movie in a suburban mall, is an adventure. We can pause on the doorstep to sniff the air, like a cat setting forth on his evening prowl, and feel the world waiting for us.

Cities coax us out. San Francisco glitters; New Orleans plays jazz. Manhattan hums with a low, intense, steady thrumming sound, like high-tension wires, or as if giants were strumming their fingers on the bridge cables; it keeps out-of-towners awake in their hotel rooms. Life is happening out there, and we're being bypassed. We dress, comb our hair, and go out to find it.

If we're rich enough, there ought to be a great, complicated, crystal chandelier suspended over the audience from a gilt dome frescoed with cherubs. The smell of damp mink stirs in the air as the audience settles its rumps more securely into the plush and rustles its programs, and the tentative squeaks and moos of the orchestra tuning up are the veritable champagne bubbles of antic-ipation, more promising than the actual overture. The houselights dim. Part of our happiness is a real expectation of liking what's to come, and part of it's simply being there where life is happening. Being *out*; being in it, sailing in the full river of it all instead of sitting earthbound and forgotten on the bank.

Or, if we're poor and rural instead, we can drive twenty miles to the Tastee-Freez in Riverton and eat soft ice cream under the daz-zling light of its parking lot, leaning against the hood of our car or pickup truck and keeping an eye out for friends and neighbors or, just possibly, an interesting stranger, rarest of all birds in Riverton.

Or hang out on a bar stool studying the labels on the bottles and waiting for someone with thick, square-cut eyelashes to say, hus-kily, hopefully, "Excuse me, is someone sitting here?"

Or hang out on a folding chair at the monthly meeting of the Historical Society, cuddling a styrofoam cup of instant coffee, sur-rounded by men in short-sleeved plaid shirts who, despite looking like underfed sheep, know an amazing lot about the Civil War, including everyone involved in Pickett's Charge.

Sometimes, everywhere, there are parties. There's the tension and drama of a party full of people we don't know, some of whom we might want to know or even go home with. Keyed up, we cruise the room sampling the strangers like canapés, cheeks flushed, adrenaline at fever pitch. Our whole lives may be changed by morning. Such parties are the amphetamine of the young and unpaired; after mating, we have a smaller stake in the game, and after aging a bit we're less optimistic.

Then there's the sociable comfort of the party of familiars, with its easy gossip. We can ask after everyone's dogs and children by name. We know our way around our hosts' music collection and can find what we want to hear; we know where the bathroom is, and the Scotch. Our lives will not change tonight, but we've mixed the excitement of going out with the security of home and the soothing pleasures of familiar faces.

The same effect could be simulated by joining a club, a club in the English sense, where we would always find someone we knew at the bar, but besides costing money, clubs in America tend to be tied more to sports than to evening sociability, and their bars and restaurants are mere extensions of their golf courses and tennis courts. Playing these games is part of the expected dues, and hanging about in the evening without having done so is a form of cheating. City clubs without golf courses are business enclaves geared to feeding lunch to clients. Sports and business: the most pervasive of American pastimes, but unsuitable for evenings out.

Evenings out are play, either because we've worked hard all day and deserve it or because we've been cooped up in the house all day and deserve it. In either case, we heard the world out there whistling for us — throwing a handful of gravel at our windows, so to speak — and said yes! wait! I'm coming.

Talking

RECREATIONAL talking is, along with private singing, one of our saddest recent losses. Like singing, talking has become a job for trained professionals, who are paid considerable sums of money to do it on television and radio while we sit silently listening or, if we're truly lonely and determined, call the station and sit holding the phone waiting for a chance to contribute our two cents' worth.

I'm told there are residual pockets of private talk left, in the Ozarks and in nursing homes in the deep South; graduate students converge on them armed with grants and tape recorders. It can't be long, though.

It happened quite suddenly, as these things do, and few people noticed until it was too late. A generation had grown up with passive entertainment and music too loud to talk over; they grew up with drugs that sucked the mind inward and blunted the urge to chat. Later they bought VCRs and invited friends over to watch movies.

Oh, they talk, of course, but not for fun. They talk about their grievances, called "therapy," and their anger, called "venting," and their relationships, called "communicating." They talk at the conference table ("brainstorming") and the kitchen table ("bonding"). But when they hear that their parents once gathered in groups of friends or relatives for the express purpose of amusing themselves and each other with talk, they're as bewildered as if we'd been sacrificing virgins at the full of the moon.

"But what did you talk *about?*"

What indeed? Sex and politics and civil rights, the best restaurants we'd ever eaten in, seven things to take to a desert island, how we'd go about faking a Jackson Pollock, what we'd do with a million dollars, what to keep in a bomb shelter, Ernest Hemingway, Julia Child, Tennessee Williams, Richard Nixon, lunatic teachers we'd had in school, cats, communism, astrology, Catholicism, the British monarchy, how we'd recast *The Wizard of Oz*, how we'd redesign the human body, a funny story about our Aunt Ellen, a funny story about our refrigerator, and shoes and ships and sealing wax and cabbages and kings. It didn't seem to matter what we talked about; if we were boring, someone would interrupt and change the subject. Indeed, sometimes half a dozen of us would talk at once, and somehow in the roiling sea of words we all mastered the delicate art of talking while simultaneously tracking several other conversations.

It was mildly competitive. A well-scored point, a clever simile, an insight — possibly prepared in advance — would be rewarded by admiration and invitations to future parties. Certain rules were understood. Saying anything, however brilliant, more than once was taboo; if we wanted more widespread appreciation, we had to rely on allies to carry our bons mots from group to group. If we waxed confessional or tearful, or complained about our spouse or our boss or our parents, it was agreed that we'd had too much to drink; our friends apologized for us and took us home. If we lapsed into power talk or intellectual superiority, nobody invited us back and we got to sit home with a good book. If we turned bellicose on the subject of *The New Yorker* or Republicans or war crimes, someone — usually the host — would step in to deflect us.

We were expected to have opinions, however wrongheaded, and defend them. Entertainingly. Above all, we were expected to entertain. That's what we were there for. This is perhaps the most difficult aspect to explain to the young, in a world where entertainment is no job for amateurs.

It was fun.

"*Fun?*"

Well, yes. Surely we all need to be listened to? Surely we all love being on stage, facing a willing, friendly, participatory audience? And surely, with all this stuff we're force-fed every day, we need to off-load it somehow? The new non-talkers, what do they *do* with their opinions; how can they carry them around, squeezed in more and more tightly in their heads? Yes, I know, you go log on with Internet and key in your thoughts on a bulletin board, but is it quite the same without faces and voices? Without even wine and chips?

After a good evening, with everyone in top form, sometimes the host would open the door and we'd stand there on the front steps and see that the streets were gray with dawn. We'd have to hurry home, shower, and dress for work, but somehow we weren't tired. We felt charged. Watching the streetlights blinking off we felt curiously buoyant, having taken in some fresh mental toys to play with and lightened our heads of a hundred thoughts.

Talking, it was called. . . .

Staying In

AS going out offers the promise of the unexpected, staying home brings the comfort of the expected. Barring unplanned calls and callers, we can tailor the evening to order. Arrange it — the popcorn, the novel, the air-conditioning or the fire in the fireplace, the VCR — and curl up in it without fear of surprises.

Some of the decision, out or in, is seasonal. On a truly evil night in January when the highways are heaped with wreckage and the sleet hisses on the windowpanes, it's a joy to call and cancel the plans and put on bedroom slippers. Back before we invented warm clothes and car heaters, nobody went out in weather like that, or certainly not for pleasure; we built a roaring fire at the mouth of the cave to discourage lions and snuggled up with each other at the back and slept until we were so uncomfortably hungry we had to go out for a mammoth. Now we try to believe that civilization has made all weathers equal, but it hasn't, and it feels best to listen to the dictates of nature and our ancestors — though the social calendar tries to subvert them by throwing most parties on the worst nights of winter.

In June, on the other hand, having to stay home feels like prison, especially for city dwellers. Those out beyond the beltways can sit in the back yard, swatting mosquitoes and exchanging pleasantries with neighbors in neighboring back yards, and be out and in at the same time, the yard being an extension of the house. They aren't off spending money in the fleshpots, but neither are they cooped up wasting the weather.

City folk get restless and claustrophobic on pleasant evenings and usually do go out, if only briefly, to relieve the pressure of being cooped. Walk the dog, buy a pack of cigarettes or a paper, pick up a movie. In winter, though, even the smallest apartment looks less like a trap and more like a refuge.

Summer or winter, once we've made the decision to go nowhere this evening, we're holding a chunk of time totally our own, an endangered pleasure if ever there was one. We can putter. File our nails, take things apart and oil them, sort photographs, tease the cat, or strive to improve our Tetris skills. We can do nothing at all, which, considering our usual frantic busyness, ought to be a rare delight but usually isn't. We've grown so unaccustomed to idleness that we can't handle it. We feel guilty, self-conscious, and a bit foolish, sitting there with our hands in our laps and our eyes glazed. Still, it's worth a few minutes of practice now and then; it's probably good for the soul. We can call it "meditating," a therapy popular a few decades ago, before we all got so strenuous.

Curiously, we aren't embarrassed by idleness while looking at television, though from a neighboring window we'd certainly appear to be idle enough. Nor can we consider it meditation, or suppose it to be good for our soul. In his 1964 tract *Understanding Media,* Marshall McLuhan warned us about it. "We become what we behold," he said. An uncomfortable thought.

Once the television habit is formed, it's hard to break. We ought to struggle against it, though, since it preempts our free time and interferes with the pleasure of our company and steals the satisfaction of doing things.

A few evenings in, calm and cozy; a few evenings out, adventuring among the muggers. Variety freshens the spirits.

Undressing

I T'S a sad commentary on our civilized lives that these clothes we spend so much time and thought and money on are so disagreeable to the human body that getting rid of them is a delight, but a delight it definitely is, and one we can indulge in daily or, rather, nightly.

Women unfasten the bra that has left pink marks on shoulder and rib cage; men untie and remove the weighty, serious shoes of the business day, shuck the strangling socks, and rub the pink marks on instep and shin. Both sexes take off wristwatches, often the massive ones currently indicative of status, that have suppressed the delicate flutter of pulse all day. (Can it be, do you think, bad for us to press these straps and chains around this most sensitive, revelatory part of our flesh, the thin-skinned, pulsing underside of the wrist? Suppose the watch is mainlining some sinister message directly into our hearts?)

Pants, skirts, suit jackets are hung away in the closet like the cares of the day; other garments are tossed into the laundry basket. Exposed skin wakes up and takes deep breaths of freedom. Air sweeps pleasantly over it. Small wonder the number of registered nudists is on the rise.

Routine undressing is always a pleasure. Undressing with a

friend as a prelude to sex can be deliriously sweet, each segment of the flesh newly exposed as a promise of the gifts to come. Still another joy is undressing because we have been forced to realize how sick we really are and to abdicate the day's work, call the office, and take to our beds.

Nakedness is irresponsibility itself, and no serious tasks are expected of the undressed. Until they put some clothes on, Adam and Eve did no work whatsoever; the minute they got dressed they had to go out and till the ground.

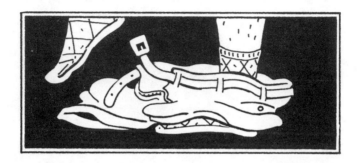

Many people, having given their skin that one brief, sweet glimpse of air and freedom, promptly lock it up again under night-gowns, pajamas, or nightshirts. Many American men are never entirely exposed except in the shower; they sleep in their undershorts. This is not recommended. It may even impose limitations on our dreams. We keep our flesh in darkness and constraint for all its waking hours, and it's cruel and unnecessary to make it sleep constrained as well. Yes, it's quite true that if the building bursts into flame in the night and the firemen break down the bedroom door with axes before we can reach for a bathrobe, there we'll be. On the other hand, the firemen have probably seen worse things in the course of their careers, and we can always keep a small rug on the floor by the bed or a dish towel on the night-table, just in case.

Bed

AS a reward for getting out of it in the morning, we're allowed to get back into bed at night; get gloriously horizontal again, after the vertical day spent carrying our bones around by ourselves.

Being so uneasy with self-indulgence, Americans tend to slight the comforts of the bed. We don't even allow ourselves to be "sick in bed" any more; we pick up a bottle of antibiotics on our way to the office, bearing flu for our colleagues. Bed is only for bedtime, and even that pleasure is being threatened in some repressive corners of the land. I read a scholarly article recently arguing that this antiquated custom of sleeping all night has come down to us from former times when we couldn't see to plow the fields in the dark. Now that we have electricity, there's no earthly reason to waste the time; we can work all night as well as all day, doing wonders for our national productivity. It's only a question of persuading employers that we don't really need the night off.

If the idea starts gaining ground, I suppose we must resort to violence.

The bed and its dressings are a fairly freewheeling, creative area of interior decor. The puritanical opt for a narrow monastic slab and a single stiff pillow, underlining the point that bed is for sleep and sleep is purely to arm us for another working day. Those who worry about their public image go in for strictly visual pleasures; carved posts and a canopy, dust ruffles, various decorative coverlets, and rows of matching ruffled pillows that contribute nothing to comfort, since they're removed before the prospective sleeper climbs in. Heaven knows who, these days, has time to arrange all this in the morning in order to take it all apart at night. The purpose, too, is elusive, since who's around to visit the bedroom in the afternoon and admire it in all its glory?

The perfect bed should be designed for a minimum of work and a maximum of horizontal relaxation. It should encourage sleep, lovemaking, reading or television-watching, and just plain lounging about, since we've arranged the rest of our homes so severely that there's no place else to get quite comfortable. In our chairs we must sit up, balancing our heads on our necks, knees bent and feet on the floor, on perpetual Red Alert. Even our couches tend to have sharply vertical arms that reject the head and neck and urge us upright again. The Romans, we were told, spent as much time as possible lying around comfortably, and look what happened to them. Sit up straight; repel Visigoths.

(Notice that you don't see any *other* intelligent mammals wobbling around all day balanced on their hind legs, or pretending to relax by sitting upright on their backsides.)

There's something on the market called a "recliner" or a "lounge chair," equipped with a lot of heavy steel struts and hinges; press a lever and a footrest shoots out, exposing steel. To discourage irresponsible lounging, these are sold as essentially therapeutic, like a prosthesis, and they look it. They're insanely, deliberately ugly — almost alarming, with overtones of the electric chair — and the usual covering is heavy plastic, icy in winter, sticky in summer. The target market is middle-aged men who have been doing something all day that requires them, for their health, to put their feet up in the evening. The rest of us should keep our feet on the floor; even our grandmother's needlepoint footstool has vanished.

For a wicked, self-indulgent while, long ago, there was the chaise longue, with a welcoming, curved back and room to stretch out the length of one's legs. You see them in antique shops. The people who buy them never, ever recline on them. Like pillow shams, they're only symbolic of comfort, to be appreciated antiseptically by the eye, not the flesh.

Consider Freud's couch. It was important, a scientific breakthrough; it became an icon. Perhaps Freud's greatest discovery, for those who hadn't already noticed, was that lying down unbuttons the soul, removes the jackboots from the inner child. Besides, it feels good.

When I was very young I used to daydream about a bedroom made entirely of bed, wall to wall, soft and springy, so that wherever you were, you were in bed, and when you were sleepy you simply closed your eyes. It was scattered with piles of picture books, pillows, stuffed bears, and some small feather comforters to cuddle into for warmth: total bed.

I still think it sounds ideal, but failing that, at least we can treat ourselves to an enormous bed — or beds, if we're married. (Why not two beds? Why all this socially enforced togetherness? After all, separate *bedrooms* were once the norm among those who could afford them, and nobody cast aspersions on their conjugal life. Let's face it, there are times when even the happiest couple doesn't want to sleep flesh-to-flesh, and if one is exiled to the living-room couch because of a fierce quarrel, a fresh head cold, or a hacking cough, that exile is going to lie there in the fetal position thinking dark thoughts about his or her loved one till three in the morning, while the one still in bed feels abandoned. Simply to repair to a separate bed is more comfortable and less punitive.)

One bed or two, it or they should be the largest that can be wedged into the room. Queen- and king-sized beds are one of the few happily luxurious innovations in our Spartan times. The unconscious mind rests better knowing it isn't balanced on a ledge, and the sleeping flesh appreciates knowing it can move around freely and needn't stay half alert to the danger of crashing into another body or falling on the floor.

In a perfect world we would all have a winter bedroom, with heavy curtains, thick rugs, and a wood-burning fireplace, and a summer one in white with flowers, or maybe on a screened porch under an apple tree, with morning birdsong. Forced to make do with just one, we must take all possible pains with its pleasures. For summer, we should have clean cotton sheets and for winter, soft flannel ones that needn't be quite so scrupulously clean; the faint scent of familiar skin is warm and welcoming.

There should always be plenty of pillows, stout ones for reading and soft ones for sleeping, and I don't care what anyone says, feather or down pillows are friendlier. The plastic-foam ones are always wilful and headstrong; try to bend or squash them into accommodation and they fight bravely, struggling to snap back to their original shape. I suspect that, aside from feather allergies, their main purpose is visual; they don't show dents, don't need plumping up. If dentlessness is what we want from a pillow, we should sleep with our heads on a saddle, like cowboys.

Children and pregnant women are being warned not to sleep under electric blankets until further studies have been completed. Personally, I feel that anything not safe enough for children, a tough tribe, isn't safe enough for me, and besides, electric blankets are always made of some stiff, scratchy, unidentifiable substance that positively dares you to snuggle up with it. I see no reason for anyone not to sleep, in winter, in the weightless world under a down comforter, a sort of semitropical wonderland that makes it much harder to get out of bed in the morning and face the realities of January. (Sometimes apartment dwellers need to open the windows to cool the bedroom enough for down, incurring the risk of waking sprinkled by an unexpected snowfall, but well worth it.) The down comforter is enclosed in an immense envelope of its own sheet; in the morning, you simply give the thing a mighty shake and let it settle, freshly plumped, back onto the bed. This is such an improvement over other styles of bedmaking that it counts as a side-pleasure all its own.

Having arranged our nocturnal comforts, we can now brush our teeth and get into them. Lie down. For the next seven or eight hours our bed will take over the tiresome duty of supporting our flesh and sleep will knit up the ravell'd sleave of care.

It's a wonder we don't do this more often. It's a wonder we manage to stay out of bed as frequently and for as long as we do.

Weekends

S ATURDAYS are practical, Sundays are sensual. Actually, Saturdays as part of the weekend have seriously eroded since women went off to work and no longer spend their weekdays picking up the dry cleaning, buying the groceries, getting the oil changed, calling the plumber, returning the library books, taking the dog to the vet and the kids for new shoes, running the vacuum cleaner, mopping the kitchen, scouring the bathtub, recycling the newspapers, addressing the Christmas cards, cleaning the fish tank, and folding the laundry. Now all these matters get pushed ahead, like snow in front of the plow, to bury Saturday, and what was once a day for picnics, sandlot baseball, and pruning roses has degenerated into a day of errands and housework. Nothing good can be said for errands and housework except the twinge of relief at having gotten at least some of them done before nightfall.

Sundays remain. They should be held sacrosanct for idle, luxurious, long-drawn-out sensual experiences, especially sex and breakfast.

Sunday-morning sex is one of the great unsung pleasures. Bedtime sex on weeknights, after a working day, with the flesh wearied and the brain frayed and confused by ordinary matters, the concentration shattered, is all very well, but on a Sunday morning, body and soul receptive as a plowed field in May, smoothed and gentled by sleep, unhurried, cradled in leisure, we can stroll through it savoring like a rajah, to the plash of offstage fountains and the harpsong of houris.

Small children who bang on the door should be threatened with death by dismemberment.

Of a Sunday, those who go to church have the added satisfaction of accomplishing their spiritual duty, but some of the idle bloom is rubbed from the day by having to put on stockings or a tie.

The central Sunday meal should take place early, as breakfast or lunch, providing a pivotal point around which the day swings gently. The French understand this principle; their Sunday lunches often last until dark and leave regiments of empty wine bottles and long naps in their wake.

Some find it acceptable at this meal for all hands to read the paper while eating, and I see nothing wrong with this since, compared to its daily version, the Sunday paper is essentially luxurious and frivolous rather than businesslike, and thus less unsociable. By choosing judiciously, it's possible to spend a long and happy day with it and never learn anything ominous. Even the most dignified paper contains splashes of color to mark the occasion; even the sections on world events are less urgent, full of reflective essays on what the past week meant instead of bulletins on today's alarms.

It's a sprawling, generous paper that comes apart into something for everyone, to be traded back and forth across the plates. (One couple I know regularly buys two copies so that each can have a crossword puzzle, but this seems wasteful and a bit unfriendly; the happily shared crossword is a benchmark of the happy marriage.)

Courteous people refrain from reading long excerpts aloud while others are busy with the funnies. Better to give a short exclamation, grunt, or chuckle, and then wait to be urged to share the piece; if nobody urges, don't.

After this central meal, it's customary to find some gentle diversion; in proper weather a spot of golf or a walk in the park, otherwise museums, art galleries, a few turns around the shopping mall or a visit with friends. Nothing essential, nothing practical: respect Sunday. Housework left over from Saturday must be left until next Saturday or perhaps until never. The thorough relishing of leisure is a reliable sign of high civilization and nothing short of appendicitis should interrupt.

The puritanical can tell themselves they're preventing burnout and storing up efficiency for the work-week ahead. The rest of us can simply loll around and tell ourselves it's Sunday.

Spring

POETS and songwriters speak highly of spring as one of the great joys of life in the temperate zone, but in the real world most of spring is disappointing. We looked forward to it too long, and the spring we had in mind in February was warmer and dryer than the actual spring when it finally arrives. We'd expected it to be a whole season, like winter, instead of a handful of separate moments and single afternoons.

In the fall we planted crocuses, because they bloom so early and don't mind getting snowed on, but somehow they're disappointing too. Not as cheering as we'd hoped. Maybe we'd secretly expected them to come up as sunflowers and hollyhocks instead of a shivering little patch of white and purple only three inches high. After we've noted the first few blooms we ignore them, and go on waiting for the moment that definitively announces spring. Some years, in some climates, it never comes at all.

The first robin doesn't count, either. Robins are dull birds, fussy and domestic, like chickens, and they don't know any more about weather than you do. I wouldn't be surprised if the whole tribe froze to death one of these springs.

After what we've been through since November, we expect the rewards of spring to be solider, more durable, than they are. The very word "April" sings in the mind like a lark, but it's notoriously unreliable. (This is certainly why it's the only month always personalized by poets as female.) On days when the sky is blue and the sun beaming, there's a vicious east wind that bites through the stoutest coat. Then it clouds over, warms up, and rains. Sometimes it snows. One morning we stroll from the house with our jacket unbuttoned and the next morning we're shoveling the driveway. Sometimes we get bronchitis. Was it for this we bothered to survive the winter? Our feelings are hurt; we feel rejected.

Some years it rains straight through May, drying out only in time for the first suffocating heat wave of June.

Still, most springs have their moments, if we stay alert to seize them. Things smell again. Only the strongest smells — diesel exhaust, woodsmoke — travel through the winter air, but in spring the nose wakes up and takes notice again, adding an extra dimension to life. Wet dogs smell, and clean laundry, and street-vendor hot dogs, and pastry shops. Sometimes we even think we can smell a bunch of pushcart daffodils; it's a thin, greenish scent, more like water than flowers, and evaporates when we try to focus on it.

In the country, spring comes with a fine, rich, rank olfactory salute of courting skunks and tomcats and the thrifty farmer spreading his fields with barn muck so urinous it makes our eyes water. We go for a walk, and the mud is deep enough to suck our boots off instead of a mere slithering over the frozen ground beneath. The color of the light changes, and the undersides of clouds are lightly smeared with purple.

In the city, invisible park-people put out rows of red tulips along a gray stone wall. Old ladies bundled in black feed breadcrumbs to the pigeons. The male pigeons puff up their feathers and circle pompously around the females, heads down, cooing in their throats like the doves that they are. Sirens and church bells sound different in the new air. Starlings clatter and racket in the twilight, which has reappeared after the abrupt nightfalls of winter and lingers smokily into evening. Alleys fill with street hockey and layup shots. Foot traffic dawdles. Hundreds of women, stripped of their winter coats, are suddenly revealed to be pregnant, as if in some merry vernal celebration of fertility. Spring did come, after all.

Then it rains for a week.

To extract the fullest pleasure from spring, it's best to keep it where it belongs, a largely imaginary season to look forward to, the light at the end of the winter tunnel, the legendary Atlantis of the year. Spring will come, we say, and the thought keeps despair at bay while we try to thaw out our pipes and start up our cars. It may not come, but it's the concept, as they say in Los Angeles, that counts.

Sports

L IFE, after we'd had a few millennia to observe it, turned out to be dreadfully unfair, so we invented sports. Sports are fair. If you or your team loses, it's because you weren't good enough to win. Your opponent played better. It may hurt, but it doesn't rankle. If you win, it's because you were better, and your victory can be savored without guilt. If you try to win by unfair means, such as stomping your opponent's groin, someone will likely notice and penalize you. Even if no one does, dishonest victories simply don't count in sports, not in any vital sense, while in real life they're just as valid as honest ones.

Coaches and headmasters praise sport as a preparation for the great game of life, but this is absurd. Nothing could be more different from life. For one thing sports, unlike life, are played according to rules. Indeed, the rules *are* the sport: life may behave bizarrely and still be life, but if the runner circles the bases clockwise it's no longer baseball. For another thing, there's a direct cause-and-effect action in sports: if A successfully does X, then points will surely, surely be scored, while in life he may do X over and over while no one even notices or bothers to chalk it up.

The fairness of it is the beauty. It consoles us for the enormous, epic, awesome unfairness of God.

Recently some people have been horrified by the bad behavior of certain sportspersons. Others have replied that they — the sports stars — were being held to unreasonably high standards, but what standards could be too high? Not because they're setting an example to the young, who are probably less pervious to example than we think, but because they're the priestly vessels through which this Ur-religion is poured, and they ought to behave with priestlike detachment. (In *Damn Yankees*, you remember, chastity was required during the season. I don't know whether it still is — it seems unlikely, these days — but I like the idea.) They shouldn't alley-cat around or gamble improperly or lose their tempers and curse in front of fans, because it ill becomes the representatives of a concept of such purity: fairness, order, justice.

I don't remember when I found out there was no Santa Claus. Perhaps I never believed in Santa Claus. I do remember when I found out that our city's teams, the gallant lads who defended our local honor like knights their fair ladies', weren't necessarily natives here and might even defend the honor of two or more cities successively; might even play *against* a town once so gallantly defended. In the same conversation I found out that they were paid for playing. Not knights at all, then, but mercenary troops without allegiance, without loyalty, without scruple. I have never forgotten the sinking horror, the sense of betrayal, and then the slow welling of cynicism: I would never be taken in again. I would never again truly believe, not in Tinker Bell nor the Redskins nor King Arthur.

I was grown before I realized that the personal loyalties and salaries of players are irrelevant, and that players exist purely as symbols — a kind of musical notation — for the poetry of order and fairness.

Sports are soothing to the chronically mistreated, who can take mental refuge in the impartiality of the rules.

They're a distraction to the unhappy, the puzzled, the pessimistic; it's highly satisfying to work up a lather over something that doesn't matter a tinker's damn. Brooding over the possibility of nuclear winter, or your lover falling in love with someone else, or global warming, or losing your job, is a dark and joyless occupation, because these things matter. How much happier to worry about beating the Steelers, the Packers, the Dolphins, the Pirates, Penn, Navy, Wilson High, or whatever, because the outcome is of absolutely no importance — unless, of course, you've bet your first-born son on it. Worrying about what doesn't matter is a highly civilized luxury and takes our mind off problems that do.

Sports played in person are said to be good exercise, and exercise is said to be one of the cardinal virtues, right up there with charity and honoring thy father. People who like exercise get additional satisfaction, win or lose, from playing a hard game of anything; they can just feel their biceps burgeoning and their pulse rates purring. Even those indifferent to their biceps can rise on the euphoric high that comes from total concentration — Zen adepts can do it staring at a spot on the wall; the rest of us need a fast round of tennis.

Public sports, though useless as exercise, nurture a community cohesion, however frail and transitory, that gives us the pleasure of belonging, of togetherness.

I lived for a while in the middle of Philadelphia, a block from Broad Street, and like most city dwellers I was totally indifferent to my neighbors except when they were throwing crockery or parties. City dwellers grow a second skin, a tough, plastic insulation, to protect themselves from the sensory assault of too many fellow humans; we pass each other on the street without a flicker.

Then the Phillies won the pennant. Won it on their home field, too, right down the street.

We hit the ground running, the whole town hit the ground running, and headed for Broad Street, up which our heroes would be riding in triumph. We milled. We were happy. We loved our neighbors as ourselves, because they too were Philadelphians. It was a warm and lovely fall night, so warm that streakers appeared almost immediately, wearing nothing but sneakers and beatific smiles. A full moon — at least it's full in my memory — illuminated a deep vault of sky full of fluffy white clouds. I met friends, people I hadn't seen in years, though they lived nearby; maybe we'd been passing each other blindly all this time and needed a Series win to recognize each other. Automotive traffic ground to a stop, baffled by the milling pedestrians, and cars neither crossed Broad Street nor proceeded along it, effectively tying up the whole center of the city. Slowly a wave of people from the stadium worked its way toward and through us, cheering. We cheered back. Trash cans were set ablaze like torches. Beer appeared. Opened cans of beer were offered from car windows and passed from hand to hand.

Reader, I drank from those beer cans. I drank the warm sudsy beer of joy, because the streets were packed with friends, the city roared with rejoicing, the moon lit up the fleecy clouds, and the Phils had won the pennant.

The next day I felt rather sheepish (see Crowds) and the *Inquirer* was distinctly snippy about those burning trash cans. But I had been there, in the thick of things, and we'd rejoiced together and for a night became indeed the city of brotherly love, and all because our boys — however flawed their characters, gross their incomes, or expedient their allegiance — had won a ball game for us.

Gardening

THE Chinese, who seem to have spent thousands of years sitting around thinking up sage proverbs, have one that says, sagely, "If you would be happy for a week, take a wife; if you would be happy for a month, kill your pig; but if you would be happy all your life, plant a garden."

Another piece of pleasure on the endangered list, at least in America; England still bursts into roses, but who here has time for all that puttering? Life is busy, life is structured, and when we aren't working we ought to be partaking of what's called "active leisure," an oxymoron if ever I heard one. Real estate ads refer glowingly to low- or zero-maintenance "landscaping." The old-time summer evening pastime of strolling the sidewalks to admire the neighbors' gardens is thinly rewarded these days. The neighbors may have set out a row of zinnias and marigolds and hired a reliable service to cut the grass and clip the hedge; they may even raise some tomatoes out back; but they haven't the time for the luxuriant burgeoning of Grandmother's day. (Heaven knows where Grandmother found the time. Perhaps by avoiding active leisure.)

The very rich still have gardens, sometimes open to the public once a year in a charitable cause, but they don't go out and *dig* in them; half the hired help would give notice if they interfered.

Possibly legions of would-be gardeners have been cowed by the creeping blight of professionalism. Garden catalogs that once trusted to our instincts now print diagrams — the lilies here, the phlox there — and offer a package of the plants we'll need to do it the correct, the professional, way. Follow the directions, water and weed, and you'll have a garden, but you aren't its artist, you're just its janitor. The once-joyous leisure pastime of creation has become a chore with rules, a job best left to qualified experts.

There are gardeners still among us, but field biologists would worry about our age group. We aren't the breeding population. It's rare, even with the best binoculars, to spot anyone under thirty elbow-deep in dirt, dividing the irises, thinning the lettuce, or dead-heading the peonies. In fact, the young seem completely mystified, as if by some obscure satanic rite glimpsed through the windows.

Non-gardeners have always been astonished at, and often contemptuous of, the amount of effort gardeners put into their gardens. They don't consider it proper exercise, either. There's plenty of exercise involved, but it's random; how can we monitor it, how can we tell — until the next morning — which muscles are receiving their due? Non-gardeners consider it work, pure and simple and unnecessary. They watch as the digger tries to stand up straight again, groaning and clutching his or her back, and wonder why anyone who didn't need to and wasn't getting paid for it would toil like that.

Gardeners too refer to it as "work": "I didn't hear the phone, I was working in the garden." We weren't, of course; gardens are so blatantly optional that whatever we do in them is play, though calling it work gives us the glow of virtue, every bit as enjoyable as the glow of sin. Calling it work means we can drop what we really ought to be doing and go out and do it all afternoon without apology.

Obviously we don't need to have a garden at all. Nobody does. We put in all that effort because the effort itself is just as much fun as the result. We're out in the fresh and pleasant air, since gardening is optional and seasonal and we needn't go out in a sleet storm to do it. It's an excuse not to waste any nice weather, too, frowsting inside folding laundry when the garden needs us. In full summer it gives us a reason to rise early to drown caterpillars and salt slugs while the dew is on the grass, then go lie in a hammock replete with accomplishment.

We can even, privately, count it as exercise, productive exercise, more acceptable to some than rowing machines, since no rowing machine ever yielded a basket of fresh peas or even a daisy.

The mind roams peacefully, since the work occupies the hands but requires only minimal attention. Usually the mind roams through next year's garden: maybe a lilac bush over there, maybe try a row of rhubarb. This gives us a comfortable sense of an attainable future under our control, or almost under it, since there's no accounting for deer, drought, or Japanese beetles. Next year shimmers in front of us in technicolor, a promise of happiness we ourselves can engineer at no more expense than a packet of nasturtium seeds. Gardening, unless you slip over the edge into fanaticism, is an inexpensive joy. As an occupation, it's never really urgent and never really finished; it waits out there for us like a game we can play whenever we want.

If we've taken good care of it, the dirt smells and feels good under our hands; the dedicated don't even mind it under their fingernails, visible proof of their industry. The early sun heats our shoulders as we stretch a length of string between two sticks to mark a straight drill for the lettuce seeds, as fine and spillable as ground pepper. It's satisfying, the order and precision of a garden early in the season, before the weeds, and once again we vow to keep it neat this year, as tidy as an allotment patch in Europe, its ground scratched daily, each plant standing on its own circle of precious damp from the daily watering can. By August, this has come to seem too much like actual work, but in May it's still a cherished vision.

We enter into a close emotional relationship with weather, and give it full attention every day: in a varied garden most of it will be good for *something* — rain for the roses, sun for the peppers, a three-day drizzle for the lettuce, a cool, tardy summer for the peas.

Anyone with a patch of dirt or a window box can grow a flower, which is rather amazing. All it takes is a paper envelope of seeds, costing a dollar or so, and these you sprinkle around, and in due course there's an actual flower where before there was only dirt. Consider all that marble Michelangelo had to buy, and haul around, and chip away at for months, while all you did was drop some black specks from an envelope. The thrill of creation, dirt cheap.

The flower itself is amazing. To our practical, task-oriented minds, it seems unnecessary for it to be so lovely and complicated and sometimes even fragrant, just in order to reproduce. *Warthogs*, after all, reproduce. I refuse to believe that the honeybee is such an exacting connoisseur as to insist on all that complex wealth of shape and color before it cooperates. No, flowers are extravagant, luxurious, probably immoral, spreading nonessential pleasure, with no respectable reason for being. It's daunting to consider how they do it, too; how they make themselves. Look at the common American wild columbine, sophisticated and intricate as a ballet — if you had to make one with your hands, out of miniature scraps of pink silk, it would take you years and drive you mad, but if you spend a couple of minutes scattering seeds, they'll make you dozens of themselves without batting an eye. Mysterious.

Vegetables, being edible, have an extra dimension of mystery and an extra justification for lallygagging around in the sunshine; surely producing food is work, not play. Never mind that we could pop into the local supermarket and buy them instead; we convince ourselves that our own, our home-grown own, are more wholesome, and certainly they do promote health, considering all the fresh air and exercise that went into them, all those hours of industrious loafing. They taste better, too, just as our own children are handsomer and brighter than the children of strangers.

They look good. A flower garden may be dazzling, but it's frivolous; a well-tended vegetable garden in July has the sturdy appeal of the useful as well as the physical grace of the curving bean, the gleam of the tightly stretched purple-black skin on an eggplant. We take a basket and pick it full of scarlet tomatoes from a place where, in spring, there was only bare ground and, like God in the world's first week, we did it ourselves. The basket is heavy with the fruits of our labor. Then we serve them for dinner. Food. *We made food.* For the rest of the family it may be just another vegetable, but for the gardener it's cause for awed self-congratulation of an order rarely found in the salaried job.

One's own flowers and some of one's own vegetables make acceptable, free, self-congratulatory gifts when visiting friends, though giving zucchini — or leaving it on the doorstep, ringing the bell, and running — is a social faux pas.

For three seasons of the year playing in the garden is an active pleasure, and then, after Christmas, the nursery catalogs arrive in the same mail with the IRS forms. Stashing the latter, we can curl up with the former. Spring moves a step closer. Green and fragrant visions open out in the mind. There's a new daylily on the market, big and yellow as a tame sun. Seven dollars will buy an infant walnut tree, and for the price of two first-run movies we can grow our own kiwi fruit; the male kiwi has variegated leaves of pink, white, and green, practically a garden in himself. Or perhaps this year we could invest in a plastic greenhouse; hideous, of course, but offering tomatoes weeks ahead of their normal coming. Or we can have raspberries, so expensive in the stores, to pick by the bucketful. A white rosebush. A gazebo.

Imaginary gardens, forever sunlit, forever free of bugs and blights, grow in the mind and gleam like Oz, promise a vernal afterlife, illuminate January. For the gardener, that is; the non-gardener still thinks they're a waste of active-leisure time.

Spending the Summer

I AM the resident curator in a small but eloquent museum of the way people used to spend the summers up until, to pick a rough date, 1981.

"Spending the summer" was what it was called, a fine, openhanded, expansive phrase. When I was a child I saw it literally: summer as a fistful of gold coins to be plunked down on the counter. The shopkeeper rang them up and handed you, in return, pretty much everything that made the rest of life worth living through.

This museum is on a mountain, along a dusty dirt road, surrounded by nothing at all except trees. Exhibits include parts of a croquet set, a first-edition Scrabble, the hook in the porch ceiling that used to hold a swing, half-a-dozen decks of cards and a sack of poker chips, three badminton rackets, a dartboard but no darts, assorted boxed jigsaw puzzles — "An English Country Garden," etc. — with pieces missing, fragments of a Monopoly game, some checkers, the complete works of Jane Austen, Anthony Trollope, and Charles Schulz, a cribbage board, a tin box of dried-up watercolors, two patched inner tubes for the river, *A Field Guide to the Birds, How to Know the Ferns,* hundreds of paperback murder mysteries, a blue Frisbee, some Mason jars with holes punched in the lids for lightning bugs, a rope hammock nibbled by mice, a deflated inflatable wading pool, a brown plastic radio, quantities of rickety folding chairs, and various straw hats and rubber boots of unknown provenance.

Sometimes I dust them.

People, even friends and relations who once spent large chunks of their summers here, gaze around in awe. "We must have been bored to death," they say. "I can't believe we stayed here for weeks and weeks. I'd go crazy here in three days."

According to the latest surveys, fewer and fewer of us are taking even the scant two-week American summer vacation these days. Instead we go away for a series of long weekends, at country inns, bed-and-breakfasts, health spas, and motels on the beach, where we play some golf or tennis, swim laps, jog, shop for antiques, or grab a quick but careful tan. The surveys don't say what we do with the children. Summer camp, I suppose. Or maybe there aren't any children anymore. And they don't say how we survive summers like 1990, when it poured rain every weekend from June till August.

Weekending degrades the whole concept of summer. Weekends we can take in any season; summer needs time. Time, in fact, is the whole point and purpose of summer, time by the armful, time heaped up and overflowing, the way it was when we were younger and schools closed down in June, revealing an expanse of time in front of us like a tree-lined allée into forever. And it takes time just to get used to time, to adjust our rhythms. Slow the pulse. Summer is cumulative and needs to pile up, attain a certain mass, at which point the days stop being days and melt together to become a place, a self-contained, motionless country wholly set apart from time and containing within its boundaries all summers past and future.

The rhythm here on the mountain was always fairly basic. The sun came up out of the valley, passed over the house, and dropped down behind the trees on the ridge. As the mountain's shadow spread into the valley, the cows in the field directly below us began to move, a moment best noted through binoculars. Very deliberately they picked their way from all over to the few worn paths, converged in a single file, and proceeded toward the barn to be milked. This was the signal for the cocktail hour to begin, and adults assembled on the deck. During the cocktail hour the shadow inched across the valley, field by field, orchard by orchard, until it was time to slice tomatoes and put the water on for the corn.

After dinner somebody read to the children, ritually, every summer, from *The Wind in the Willows* and *The Sword in the Stone,* because this had been the custom since back before I was a summer child on the mountain. The children, having spent the afternoon with a trickling hose, a saucepan, and water pistols, didn't need bathing. They fell asleep under a mulch of "Peanuts" books. Then the owls tuned up.

That's about it, I'm afraid. Sometimes a restless soul would go for a walk and come back with wineberries or ditch flowers. Sometimes a child would catch a toad or turtle for which housing had to be found. Occasionally a male guest would assert his machismo by mowing the lawn; this entitled him to spend the rest of the day in the hammock with a can of cold beer on his chest.

As I finish my spiel, museum visitors shake their heads in wonder, pretending to admire those generations for their endurance of such boredom, but secretly they're shocked. In just a decade or so, idleness, once a summer perk, has become a social sin and slightly disgusting, like eating whipped cream with your fingers.

Some people summered at the beach, and this rhythm was more complicated: morning swim, shower, lunch, nap, afternoon swim, shower, drinks, dinner. Sand in the bathtub. Beach towels on the line. Citronella candles for the mosquitoes. Breeze off the water. The principle remained the same: the rhythm needed to be repeated day after day until it soaked into the very flesh and turned into the country called Summer. Students of Eastern religions will note the similarity to the cyclical repetition of Buddhist prayers until they take on an independent life and momentum of their own. No good Buddhist expects to accomplish this over a long weekend.

Once, before we got fully accustomed to air-conditioning, even summer in the city had its rhythms. For millennia we'd taken it for granted that everything slowed down in hot weather, and we strolled and dawdled. Lounged around the watercooler and left work early; no use trying to drum up business, everyone's out of town. We licked ice-cream cones, picnicked on the fire escape, and got grass stains on our trousers at concerts in the park. Then we and our employers finally absorbed the message of air-conditioning: there is absolutely no reason to loll around in August, no excuse for idleness. Besides, while making it so much pleasanter indoors, air-conditioning has made the outdoors rather horrid. The summer idler sits on his front steps rocked by the pulsing roar and fetid breath of a million room-coolers, like the invasion of an army of dragons. Might as well go inside. And inside, we can't tell summer from winter. If there were birds singing, we couldn't hear them.

Of course, there are several sound reasons for the decline of summer. We work more than we used to, though nobody seems quite sure why, and because we're doing it we've convinced ourselves that it's good. Purposeful activity is a virtue and doing nothing is a vice. Besides, if we took a long vacation, without beeper or laptop, we might seem, in our own eyes, less busy and therefore less important. Less good.

From the mid-sixties through most of the seventies it was widely believed that people who worked too hard were either contemptible greedheads or just not very good at their jobs. Leisure was better for the soul, and the soul was important. This notion suffered a total reversal in the eighties, and now our small available free time should be spent in the most strenuous possible activity, because this means we're *not doing nothing*. We're not sloshing aimlessly around in the swimming pool just because it's cool and pleasant; we're swimming laps, counting as we turn.

Another factor is the flood of mothers into the more businesslike zones of the workforce. Unlike schoolteachers, lawyers don't take their kids to the beach for a month; it would undermine the gross national product.

Still, there are more civilized countries, successful countries, industrialized countries, where summer is respected and all citizens have a right and a duty to spend much of it in outdoor idleness.

Once bulging with summer people, the little museum on the mountain sits waiting now, except on weekends. But even weekend guests, accustomed to the brisker life, get restive. They aren't here long enough to adjust their rhythms, and presently they drive over to the Appalachian Trail and hike back and forth on it, in the company of other hikers, because this is purposeful exercise, unlike wandering around the dirt roads picking Queen Anne's lace. Unlike reading murder mysteries in broad daylight. Unlike lying in a hammock looking up at the lacework of leaves and trying to stay awake, because if we fall asleep we might miss the hummingbird's next trip to the feeder, or even the cows on their way to the barn and the onset of cocktail hour.

I keep all in order, though. America has a short attention span, fads come and go, and it may be that we'll get tired of all this activity and the days of summer idleness will return. People will come back to spend long, dateless, motionless chunks of time on the mountain.

They'll find everything still waiting for them — the blue Frisbee, the poker chips, *How to Know the Ferns,* the wading pool, the straw hats, the jigsaw puzzles. I keep them dusted.

The Fourth

HENRY James has written, "A large appetite for holidays, the ability not only to take them but to know what to do about them when taken, is the sign of a robust people, and judged by this measure we Americans are sadly inexpert."

We should take heed, and celebrate our feast days more merrily. But perhaps James, an intellectual by trade, was in the wrong place for the Fourth, or maybe firecrackers hurt his ears. Americans relish the Fourth.

The Fourth of July may be our happiest holiday. A surprising number of adults, rummaging for cloudless childhood memories, come up with Fourths instead of Christmases.

Christmas has its dark shadows of greed and disappointment, and being sectarian, it can sever us temporarily from friends and lovers of other sects. New Year's has its hangover, Easter its purple jelly beans tasting of guest-room soap. Labor Day is a mystery to everyone under fifty, and coincides with the real or remembered beginning of school. Halloween is for children, cross-dressers, and vandals; Thanksgiving is for eating far more bland, uninspiring food than we ever wanted to eat. But the Fourth of July is a solid joy of a holiday, the crown of summer, the jingle of gin-and-tonic, the bang of boys, the tootle and thump of the volunteer fire department's marching band, and even the smallest children get to stay up past their bedtime.

Everyone loves it except the family dog, under the bed quaking like an aspic.

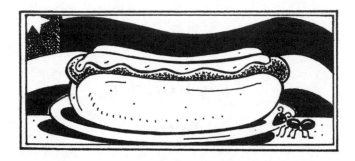

It's even a decent reason to dance and sing, since military victories — even if we couldn't have done it without the French — are always rousing, and independence (see GROWING UP) is always fun, if a bit moot in this case. Without Hong Kong, Britain runs no more colonies and is now merely poor little England, overrun with tourists and scorned by some as a theme park with muggers; even if we hadn't won the war we probably wouldn't still be paying taxes on her tea.

Never mind, ring out the bells and fire the Roman candles — we won, we're free.

Another joyful aspect of the day is its malleable nature. It's hard to talk your way out of Halloween candy, Thanksgiving turkeys, Hannukah candles, Christmas trees, or Easter eggs, but we can shape the Fourth however we please.

One good way to celebrate is to find a small town within driving distance, population anywhere between six hundred and ten thousand, and crash its party. Ideally this should be under the auspices of the volunteer fire and rescue department, which should have a ladies' auxiliary, which should be having a bake sale and providing potato salad for the Scouts or the Little League, which should be peddling lemonade and hot dogs. (Hot dogs are no doubt as poisonous as everyone says, but on this special day nothing replaces their combination of textures — the squish of the bun, followed by the rubbery resistance of the hot dog's skin, followed by its familiar mealy interior and classic childhood flavor.)

Nothing is expected of the drop-in guest; just stand around covered with mustard, applaud the parade, and wait for dark and fireworks.

Here on the mountain, it's a good thing to have some friends gather on the roof, with a fine view of the valley and the fireworks of three small towns. At this distance, though, we miss the impact of the booms, which should tickle the soles of one's feet and vibrate in the chest cavity. And we miss the smell. Whatever the chemical components in the smell of fireworks, it elates the blood and makes horses prance and little boys run in circles yelling aimlessly.

Home fireworks used to be splendid and dangerous and light up the sky, but now that we worry so obsessively about safety they've shrunk; in serious-minded states even the dimmest are illegal. And they're not very good any more. Half of them are duds and the rest sizzle only briefly in a sprinkle of orange sparks. Their only real kick is illegality. We buy them in another, more freewheeling state and smuggle them home, celebrating our national independence on a small, personal scale, thousands of us otherwise law-abiding citizens with the trunks of our cars full of Shower of Delights and Rainbow Fountains. If we ever get rear-ended, how we'll twinkle.

Out in the countryside, according to the rural wisdom, corn should be knee-high by the Fourth of July. Those who have coddled their tomato plants look to have the first tomatoes for the picnic. There may be family reunions, sprawling over the house and yard or the civic park, with softball games, coolers of beer, yellowjackets and gassy whiffs of charcoal-lighter fluid, babies napping in the shade on quilts. Flags should be flown, even by those normally suspicious of patriotic symbols. Revolutionary War re-enactments should take place, marked by a profusion of tents and men in musty-smelling period uniforms brandishing long, spidery guns.

The sun should shine. There should be plenty of bright, hot sunshine, now, before we've had our fill of it in the ovens of August. Children should rejoice because school vacation is now officially signed and sealed and goes cartwheeling on ahead without end through the leafy caverns of summer. Where there are pools, lakes, or beaches, everyone should swim.

It's the queen of holidays. May your tomatoes always ripen in time for it and no thunderstorm ever delay your parade.

Plans

THE difference between plans and mere daydreams is the amount of work that goes into plans. Ideally, plans should have some basis in possibility, however remote; to buy a piece of land in the country, build a house on it, and raise llamas, for instance, or design a houseboat on which to retire, or spend three months in Italy. Theoretically possible. We might win the lottery, after all. Somebody has to win it, and how embarrassing to be caught planless and have to tell the reporters that, beyond paying off our credit cards, we can't imagine how we're going to spend $8 million.

These should be plans that require creative thinking, unlike planning to send the kid to college or buy a new car, which needs only some comparison shopping and a bank loan or second mortgage. The more elaborate the plan, the more satisfying. Make scale drawings and work out detailed itineraries; study maps; send away for packets of information. If the plans involve another person, argue. Disagree over the best place to put the bathroom or the best paths for a walking tour of the Lake District. Keep folders of notes and information, shelves of books; build models out of matchsticks. During slow periods at the office, doodle a few refinements. Make lists of the camping equipment needed for the safari.

Like the gardener's future garden, plans are fail-safe and trouble-free as long as they stay plans. Any miscalculations we've made don't matter; the imaginary houseboat never sinks.

Over the months or years, the carefully erected plan takes on an independent reality of its own. The unwritten novel, the driftwood shack in the Florida Keys rise up and exist in another dimension. We can almost touch them. The noonday wine at the *pensione* bleeds through the tuna sandwich we're actually eating; who's to say which is the dream?

Due to the nature of the world, most of us can't have everything we want. Disciplinarians urge us to resign ourselves and rest content with the possible. Plans, however, are cheap, and don't gang aft a-gley unless we actually buy the land in the country or put the boat in the water. They give us heart, broaden our days, and sing to us from around the corner of the future. Without them, who would support the lottery? And how will we know what to do when we win?

Travel: Getting There

I N the past thirty years or so, travel has gotten faster, less interesting, and much less fun. Compare an overnight coach flight to Heathrow with sailing to Southampton on the *Normandy*. Compare the plastic airplane dinner or the highway hamburger with lunch on the Orient Express.

By land, trains are the best way to travel. In America they've fallen into sad times of late, and those who remember their golden days are always grieved by the dirty windows, microwaved snacks, shabby cars, and rickety tracks. Advanced high-tech or high-luxe in Europe and Japan, trains here, especially in the East, are almost extinct and they look it. Still, even here, even now, they're the only way to travel if we're traveling to see what's out there in the world.

From a plane, the view often looks like the inside of an old mattress, and even when you can see the ground it has less to do with the place itself than a road map does; at least a map names the towns and rivers. Some of it's spectacular, I admit, like that first view of the home continent when we're coming back across the North Atlantic. Whatever that country is (in a plane, you needn't even know what *country* you're in, or over) that spreads out so brown and endless, spotted with blue lakes, or puddles, and sharply ruled by what must be roads, except that no real road was ever so long and straight and futile, arrowing across nowhere from nowhere to nowhere; fascinating but abstract. We can hardly call it travel if we don't know what we're looking at, any more than we can guess the purpose of those giant circles in Wyoming — or is it

Utah? We might as well stay home and admire the patterns in a kaleidoscope.

Except for the idle rich and the busy executive, planes are desperately uncomfortable to sit in, and there's no alternative to sitting. Except on Air France, the food seems like a form of punishment, and we always vow to pack a lunch the next time and the next time we forget. When we land, we're still many miles from our destination and have to grapple with ground transportation. Planes are fast, and that's all that can be said for them; it's a big country and we're in a hurry. Our pleasure on a plane is limited to anticipation of the journey's end — i.e., getting off the thing. They're a means to an end, without charm or ambience, and the last of their glamour vanished just after Bogart shoved Bergman aboard.

Car travel on our vaunted interstate system is even worse. At least on a plane they don't make you drive.

Once, back when the purpose of roads was to link one Main Street with another, driving was an intimate adventure through the real world, and families piled into the car on weekends to "go for a drive" and look at other places and people. Driving was slower then, but people didn't expect it to be faster. They expected to poke along behind a truckload of watermelons, pass it, and then have to repass it after they'd stopped at a roadside diner for coffee and a chat with the waitress. On vacation journeys they expected to see many Main Streets, sometimes with a couple of dogs asleep in the intersection, sometimes with speed traps. They dawdled along reading signs for church socials and criticizing the washing hung on a line. They stopped for gas and a freckled teenager scouring the windshield told them that 23 had a bridge washed out between here and Valdosta and they'd better take 11 instead. It took days to get from here to there, especially with small children needing to pee and sometimes a flat tire, but it was real travel all the way.

Now we have superhighways and supercars. Bulleting down the road, there's nothing to see but trucks and cars. In the interests of beautification the sides of the road are planted with vegetation that looks the same in every state and may or may not be organic in origin. Some places allow billboards, and these are a glad relief and respite from crushing boredom. Persons of a competitive nature relieve their boredom by outrunning and outmaneuvering the competition in high-speed games of car hockey. Our only sense of change and motion comes from the different radio stations that fade in and out as we rip through their territories. From time to time a sign tells us we've changed states and should drive carefully, which helps to orient us: if this is Pennsylvania, that must have been Ohio.

It's efficient, but like planes it isn't elsewhere, just a limbo on the way to elsewhere. For some, perhaps especially for men, it has the advantage of being their own limbo, their own beloved car under their personal control, a movable, walled section of their defensible turf, though passing through the turf of strangers. For them, travel by car postpones the disorientation of being a stranger in a strange land; the journey hasn't truly begun till they get out from behind the wheel. (Perhaps this explains the appeal of motels, with one's familiar car reassuringly close at hand.)

Stepping into a train, on the other hand, you were instantly away from home. The adventure began at once. The train is, or was, a pleasure in itself. Train stations in major cities were palaces of hushed anticipation; those in small towns were shining gateways to the great world. People smiled in train stations. Nobody smiles in O'Hare.

The modern train-traveler sits down and gropes, baffled, for a seat belt, and then gradually adjusts to the glad freedom of traveling unstrapped. The hoarse cries of " 'Board!" still echo down the platform as they always have and tingle in the blood.

Trains are the basic metaphor for travel. Songs about them are a whole sub-genre. Ask the farm boys on the great plains who used to lie in bed and listen to the train whistle across the wheatfields, longing and longing to be aboard and traveling toward a city, any city. A jet trail marked on a blue sky may be pretty, but it lacks the visceral tug of the train. It's too far away; there's no road between you and it. Ask the kids who waited by the tracks and at the whistle-stops just for the flash of windows going by, the flicker of travelers' faces, and smiled wistfully and waved. Ask anyone old enough to remember the glitter and jingle of the dining car, everyone's most exciting eatery, with a flower in the vase and the world clicking by outside.

The world is mysteriously improved by being framed in a train window. It looks more important. Even gritty industrial slums quiver with meaning. Every train-traveler has packets of sharply remembered mental snapshots: an old man on a sagging porch, sitting beside a refrigerator watching the train. A beaver dam in a forest in Virginia. The couple in the white convertible, stopped at a grade crossing, laughing. Sunset over Manhattan. Wild swans on a lake. I remember the round, brown hills south of Los Angeles, massed like sleeping pigs, and a single small, faraway house on one of them, with a mile or two of road that switchbacked up to its door and stopped. It seemed urgently, supernaturally real. It still does. Everything from a train window has the feverish reality we yearn for when we travel.

From a plane, the world is a toy, or a riddle, or gray fluff. In a car, the presence of the highway itself has altered local reality, and besides, at that speed we'd best keep our eyes on the road. Only trains bring us the great elsewhere between home and destination, and explain the idea of distance, so that when we get there we know we're away.

Travel: Being There

THE pleasure of being elsewhere is in being impressed, in the basic sense of the word; in absorbing an impression, like clay under a thumb; in being imprinted with the vividness of small things simply because we found them when we were away from home. Differentness fills us like a kind of magic dinner, and fleshes out our senses. The hee-haw of an ambulance in the foreign streets sings with a pure and alien glamour, quite unrelated to the irritating scream of emergency vehicles back home.

Once referred to as "a change of air" or "a change of scene," travel was the prescribed cure for melancholy, broken hearts, non-specific boredom, mysterious illnesses, and young people set on unsuitable matches. (Franklin Delano Roosevelt's mother took him off on a cruise so he'd forget about marrying Eleanor. It didn't work.) Strangeness snatches at our attention, and it feels good. Change feels good. It's why we watch a parade, because it changes, passing by; nobody wants to hang around watching a parade stand still.

It's hard to admit we're traveling just to look at something different, so we need to say we need to travel. If we can convince ourselves that we're seriously stressed from hard, responsible work, we can go spend two weeks lying in the broiling sand somewhere doing nothing, so that we'll be all the more efficient when we get back to the office. In Calvinist societies, anything that improves our work lives needs no apology, even if it involves dancing girls, sun poisoning, and piña coladas.

This isn't really, in any sense of the thought, travel. Probably we could have more cheaply and just as effectively stayed at home with a sunlamp, a local prostitute, and a bottle of rum, but it wouldn't have sounded as therapeutic or impressive to our colleagues afterwards, and our photographs would have lacked panache.

We wouldn't have enjoyed it as much, either. Being *away* is part, or most, of the point. Besides, your really serious, mature adult doesn't get involved with rum and sunshine at home. For some things, you have to leave town.

The rest of us can say we travel for educational purposes, because it broadens our view and gives us a whole new perspective on our work. Or we can come clean and admit we just want to see, and eat, and listen to, something nondomestic for a change: we go because we want to be somewhere else.

Those of us with active consciences will be happiest after we've done the obligatory and paid our respects to the cathedrals, monuments, and museums, and, duty accomplished, can turn our wondering eyes to how the light seems different, brighter or softer or more golden, and how a cat asleep on a doorstep looks like a painting, a marvel of a cat, the very essence of France or Italy or Guadalajara or Nantucket, utterly different from similar cats on doorsteps back home: we take its picture.

We're dizzy with the marvelously ordinary lives lived elsewhere, by creatures apparently unaware of being exotic; they buy bread, engage in traffic jams, and quarrel on park benches as if they thought they were nothing unusual. Entranced, we watch them scratch and yawn, try on hats, light cigarettes.

Years from now we'll have trouble calling up the splendor of the gothic apse, but we'll never forget the square beside the cathedral where we drank coffee and fed scraps of pastry to a scruffy yellow dog, a *foreign* dog, his unremarkable face etched in memory. We even remember the weight and texture of the coffee cup, exotic as Tibet.

Everything has a peculiar clarity and significance because we aren't going to be here long. In a few days or weeks we'll leave, go home where we needn't notice things because they will always be available to notice, but here we must seize the chance; we'll never see this dog, this square, this coffee cup again.

Small, odd things happen away from home, or things that seem odd or remarkable because we aren't on our own turf, where they might be unnoticed or even irritating. In San Juan, a friend and I were eating lunch in the street, at a table set out unsteadily on the cobblestone roadway. When a car wanted to go by, the waiter, without apology, picked up our table and moved it out of the way, we carried our chairs. The car went by; our lunch furniture was replaced on the street. We were very pleased, simply because this would probably not have happened in Cleveland or St. Louis or Philadelphia.

A beggar in Madrid is more charming, has more intelligent and liquid eyes, than a beggar in Manhattan; a broken-down bus in Turkey is more exciting than a bus with similar transmission problems in Boston.

We taste the different food, and it's more than merely good or bad, it's *their* food. Other food. Even dismal messes in a provincial British pub are uniquely, Britishly dismal. Glamorously dismal. We eat respectfully, filling up with otherness. Soggy English sausage rolls, rubbery Italian squid, painful Mexican chiles.

The bed is damp and lumpy and the food overcooked, it's raining, but look, look out the window! We're in north Wales, and the ruin on the mountain facing us is very ancient, almost certainly haunted by unquiet pre-Christian spirits. In the pub, men are actually teasing the barmaid in Welsh: *they live here.* Perhaps they'd rather live in London, or even in Baltimore; probably they know something prosaic about that ruin; we must be careful not to ask.

We want to believe everything. It helps us extract the richest juice from the journey; we want to be gullible, not skeptical. Let there be ghosts and heroes, saints and dragons, wherever we go. We're here for fantasy, not fact. We've left nine-tenths of our identity back home with our familiar furniture, and it makes us a little lightheaded.

Foreign places tend to stay in the mind, alert and well lit, curiously stirring compared with where we live, no matter how satisfactory home may be. *I was in Brittany*, I think, and there it is, a cliff over the sea, webbed with chalk paths. A week in dragonfly season steering a narrowboat through its canals, with fishermen on the banks, Breton fishermen, stamped with so much more character, more personalness, than anyone who ever dropped a line into my home Shenandoah. There was a woman who brought her heap of white washing down to the canal in a wheelbarrow and pounded it on a board in the shallow, dirty water. She waved at us. I can see her now. *I was in Denmark*: it was a long time ago, but there are still cornflowers and poppies at the edges of its fields, and in front of me, on a bus, a fat woman is still smoking a pre-breakfast cigar. I think of the silliness of Monaco, the seriousness of the English midlands, the size of the Alps, the expanse of west Texas. I remember my first morning in San Francisco, raging drunk with exhilaration up and down its steep streets, a Valhalla of a city. I remember the pitiless puritanical light north of Boston, a searching light as sharp as church steeples, peering into the very bloodstream.

I remember the iodine smell of the Atlantic, intoxicating to all Easterners, different from all the other oceans. It's best appreciated driving toward it in summer through the Jersey Pine Barrens, where the strong, raunchy, sea smell gradually overtakes and then replaces the spicy smell of hot pine needles.

There's nothing wrong with where I live, but remembering these things makes me peculiarly happy.

I don't often get to go places, so everywhere I go feels like Christmas morning. The rich who go everywhere report that there gets more and more like here, and they're bored and irritated, and complain that the posada on Lake Chapala has changed management and Tierra del Fuego was crawling with Japanese dwarfed by life-threatening cameras; these may be the same new management and the same Japanese they ran across in Singapore and Stratford-upon-Avon. And if the trend toward universally standard architecture and international purveying chains continues, there will be no further point in traveling.

Perhaps we should go everywhere soon.

Travel: Taking Pictures

I LIKE taking pictures away from home, but for years I was ashamed of carrying a camera, though not nearly so ashamed as some of my companions, who couldn't have felt worse if I'd traveled with an anteater around my neck. Mere tourists, not proper travelers, carry cameras. Proper travelers record with their eyes, remember with their brains and senses, absorb the essence of the place unfiltered through extra equipment. The camera impedes concentration. It comes between the observer and the observed. It serves up a contrived, falsified vision of the reality.

Knowing this, I took pictures anyway, but guiltily. Then the video camera came along. It was bigger, more obtrusive, more vulgar, more technologically advanced. It made my modest still camera much less offensive, almost quaintly old-fashioned, almost charming.

Those who don't take pictures maintain that those who do simply want to bore or impress their friends back home, but I hotly dispute this. I think we take them for ourselves; travel gives us fresh eyes, and we're trying to bring some of the freshness back home to keep. Greedily, we expect to own a few pieces of this different place, personalized souvenirs to carry away like towels from the hotel.

It's true that some photographers view being elsewhere as a chance to take pictures of their companions against novel backdrops. "There is Sally in front of the Taj Mahal; this is Mum on a camel, Bill in a grass skirt, me and the Washington Monument." These people are perhaps timid travelers, uneasy so far from home base and stabilizing themselves with the known face in the foreign scene, to prove that though away they are not adrift.

Purists, however, shove Mum aside; her they can see back home. Let no element of the familiar intrude on the strange.

The first roll of film traditionally records the important facts of the place, the castle, the waterfall, the mountains as seen from one's hotel room. This is the equivalent of doing the cathedral before sitting in the piazza. The following rolls are for fun, for relishing the there-ness; the cat-on-the-doorstep shots. Having dutifully recorded the castle, we can dally a while to shoot the shaggy purple flowers growing so improbably from the chinks in its stones. These pictures will mean nothing to anyone but the photographer, but whose pictures are they, anyway?

The journey over, we go home. With luck our furniture awaits us, the cat didn't run away, the dog survived the kennel, and no Goldilocks is asleep in our bed. We empty our suitcases into the washing machine and drop off our sackful of pictures to be developed.

They're disappointing. Somehow we'd expected the entire journey to rise like a genie from the envelope, but it doesn't. We ruffle through them and they seem curiously flat, not as rich and flavorful as we'd imagined them. Instead of enhancing our memories they seem to be sucking the juice from them, siphoning off the smells and sounds, shrinking the mountains. Sadly we put them away.

Stuffed in a box, they change and grow. Three years later we take them back out and lo, the genie rises. Instead of sucking out flavor, they pour it in. There's the stone walkway to the train station in Villefranche; Mediterranean light suddenly surrounds us. These are the rocks; I remember, I was there, it was hot and smelled of wild thyme and suntan lotion. See the sheep-tufted slopes in Snowdonia; the rest of the countryside, beyond the picture, opens out on all sides in rolling emerald hills to the horizon, and sheep calls to sheep. How pleasant to be there again so quickly and cheaply.

When I was a child you could buy, at the ten-cent store, a handful of dusty-looking pebbles that you dropped into a special solution, and mysteriously they grew into a tiny, brightly colored forest of complicated branchy spikes, like coral. Even so, the travel pictures in the solution of time.

Probably we should have them developed and stow them directly in the box, without opening the envelopes, and let them ripen for a year or two.

Visiting

"G O often to the house of thy friend," says a Scandinavian proverb, "for the weeds soon choke the unused path."

Visiting is a pleasure; being visited is usually a mixed or ambivalent joy. The visitee, unless he or she is unusually self-confident, probably felt it necessary to clean up the house or at least unhook the dirty socks from the lampshades and swab the sticky patch on the kitchen floor. Food had to be bought and cooked, possibly expensive or quirky food to accommodate the visitor's latest dietary fad. The sheets on the guest bed had to be changed and clean towels ferreted out. And once ensconced, the visitor may come to seem like occupying troops and possibly permanent. The visitee is helpless: nice people don't throw guests out into the street because their airspace feels crowded and they're tired of thinking up entertainments. The visitor can always go home; the visitee is already home, trapped like a rat in a drainpipe.

Still, there are compensations. There's the excuse from duties: "I can't, I have guests" is accepted everywhere. There's conversation, too often neglected with your usually available housemates. There's the chance to splurge on outings, to drop everything and take the guests to places where you wouldn't take yourself, to parks and gardens and landmarks and the theater. And of course, if you've laid in some really nice bottles of wine, you, too, get to drink them.

For visitors, at least for those of the female sex, it's almost all candy.

Deep down, a man in his own home still feels that he's there to be taken care of, while a woman at home feels that she's there to take care of everyone and everything in the whole place. The back of the mind is never quite free of duties, always alert to the supplies of coffee, clean laundry, and toilet paper; the necessity of answering the phone, opening the mail, closing the windows, feeding the cat, watering the plants. Away, the irresponsibility is the purest of luxuries.

Food, drink, and a bed have been provided. If the dog throws up on the rug, it isn't our dog or our rug. If the house catches fire we have only our suitcase to rescue. If it rains on our plans, it's our host who feels guilty. Our only duty is to be suitably grateful and, after the specified time, go away. For a brief, blissful interlude we aren't in charge of ourselves or our meals, let alone the vagaries of plumbing and electricity. We needn't even know the local train schedules and phone numbers. Affably we smile and wait to be driven around to see the sights. It's the perfect mix of excitement and security, adventure and the womb.

A well-tended list of friends and relations should cover a variety of places, because visiting is a cheap and carefree way to see the world; all we need provide is plane fare or gasoline. We should cultivate a network of couches in exciting cities, peaceful country-sides, and foreign lands, on ski slopes or beaches or lakes. Equipped with a good bedroll, we're ready to descend even on those who prudently don't own a full-length couch.

The flaws are minimal. In the case of the proper guest bed, we're expected to put it back together in the morning, and often it's a complicated construct. People who themselves sleep in Spartan simplicity will go hog-wild doing up the guest room, and there we are, in the rosy light of dawn, faced with the pile of complicated doodads we yanked so recklessly off the bed last night and must now reassemble. All we can remember is that the blue embroidered thing went crosswise in a diamond shape instead of four-square. Unless that was the patchwork piece, and the embroidered bit went under it.

Even with only the usual dressings, the guest bed resists making. Like a horse or a violin in the hands of strangers, it fights off our alien touch. The top sheet hangs down two feet on one side and two inches on the other. The coverlet, no matter how many times we circle it tugging, will never come out even, and by now our back hurts. The bed looks as if we were still in it. After twenty minutes we give up, close the door tightly, and go down to breakfast, nerves frazzled.

One woman I know lays her sleeping-bag down very gently on top of all the guest arrangements, and in the morning rolls it up again, smooths out the odd wrinkle, and greets the day smiling.

Some of our friends, bored with the ordinary taps that control one's shower so easily and efficiently, have invested in industrial-strength postmodern bathing machinery. Check ahead of time, or you will find yourself naked and shivering, or scalded, or bone dry, wrestling with an outsized steel gearwheel that won't do anything you ask. If you don't recognize what you're looking at, sponge off with a washcloth or the corner of a towel.

The other drawback is the kitchen in the absence of the hosts, who may have gone off early to work. It's a well-known peculiarity of the human race that no two people arrange their eating equipment similarly. It may seem sensible to A to keep cups and glasses in the handiest cupboard, the one to the right of the sink, but when he opens B's right-hand cupboard he finds instead a spare roll of paper towels and the Christmas punchbowl. The drawer that should logically hold spoons and forks contains plastic wrap and bits of string, and the coffee is simply nowhere to be found, because B keeps it in the freezer where A will never think to look.

These small flaws aside, visiting is delightful. Even the briefest visit, for lunch or tea or drinks, glows with the joy of having someone else in charge and doing all the work.

Of course, in return we get visited, and pushed out onto the limb of responsibility for food, drink, entertainment, and decorative doodads on the guest bed, but such is life. We console ourselves with sweet dreams of retaliation, and an even longer stay next time.

Boats

I WAS at an important meeting on the twenty-third floor. The top brass of the agency was there, and the CEO of its biggest client, flanked by his lieutenants, and we were hammering out the future of its advertising in spite of the rather distracting view, for the appreciation of which the agency had fixed a small telescope to the windowsill.

The agency brass unfurled the layouts. We all leaned forward attentively. Then I jumped up, overturning my chair, and cried, "Oh, look! *Look!*" and ran to the window. The *Queen Elizabeth 2* was coming in.

All the brass jumped up. We struggled for possession of the telescope and, as the only woman present, I won, briefly.

The decks were bulging with passengers, all watching the arrival as happily as we were. I saw them waving; I could make out their faces. I panned along the decks, peering intently, and realized that I was irrationally hoping to find myself among them, my own face in the crowd of passengers.

Romantically speaking, ship travel is to plane travel what a harbor is to an airport. Nobody runs to the window to see a 747 taxiing up to its gate.

Cruise ships don't count. I've never been on one, but by all reports they're not travel so much as movable resorts, floating parties, and their pleasures could be fully savored without their bothering to leave port. Cruise ships are advertised as the perfect venue for romance, though it's left a bit vague as to whether you should bring your own or look for it on board. Still, there's something a bit, well, *deliberate* about the cruise-ship fling. Too well publicized, too self-conscious; romance is what you paid for. Those using a ship for transportation — and as late as 1970 it was still a legitimate way to travel — found romance as an accidental bonus, pretending it took them by surprise.

Back before laptops and the interfering telephones connecting traveler with home and office, the passenger was gloriously isolated from the daily world of deadlines, annual reports, and even loved ones left behind. Morality springs from a context of society and community which, in mid-Atlantic, seemed long ago and far away. Lacking the frantic, organized entertainment of the cruise ship, cut off from the eyes of the world, reasonably certain of a destination that would separate lovers and limit consequences, sea travelers coupled indiscriminately, merrily, comfortably.

Making passionate love to your seatmate on the red-eye from Los Angeles is not a comparable option.

On my first journey out of the country I crossed (obsolete verb meaning to go from America to Europe or vice versa at sea level) on the cramped and bumpy little *Stavangerfiord*, full of students with guitars and impoverished professors with large families traveling on sabbatical. The cabins were so tiny only one person at a time could stand in the floor space to dress. The food was utilitarian — the reindeer patties, provided as ethnic color, were quite nasty.

If you were at all polite to the officers you were invited to climb up on the bridge and look at the radar screen and the narrow deck pitching and shifting far below, and know you were *at sea*. You were *crossing the ocean*. Ahead was Copenhagen, and you had idle days and days to think about it shining over the horizon like the North Star.

We made our own entertainment. A girl with long hair sat cross-legged on the floor of the lounge and played folk songs on her guitar, and we sang along. We sang all the great ship songs. We sang the *Titanic* song, roaring the chorus:

> *O it was SA-AD when the great ship went down*
> *To the BOTTOM of the sea*

A ship's officer burst into the lounge and shouted furiously at our girl in Norwegian. Blushing, she put away the guitar and we all fell silent, namelessly guilty. Later I asked the English-speaking bartender what was wrong, and he shrugged. "They're all superstitious, sailors," he said. "It was bad timing. We were right over the place where it happened."

I tingled, pleased; this was travel with tradition behind it and stories to tell. Travel with its watery roots going back to Leif Eriksson.

Nobody takes a guitar on a plane to sit in the aisle singing about plane crashes. There are no songs about plane crashes; they're anti-romantic. Dropping out of the sky in a plane is entirely disagreeable to consider, while a sinking ship offered lifeboats and the possibility of being marooned on a palm-fringed isle with a charming stranger.

Later, richer, I crossed on the *France,* most airy and elegant of ships, but the food was too good. It was distracting. It's hard to absorb the fact of being at sea when all you can think about is lunch.

Even now, people with plenty of time can book passage on a freighter, but from the passenger's point of view it's just a plain-clothes cruise ship, moving from port to port, loading and unloading. And crossing on the QE2 isn't transport so much as a curiosity, a quaintly old-fashioned experience for the very rich. And even she spends most of her time aimlessly island-hopping. Planes are here to stay.

We still have small boats, though, for fun, not travel, and they have their own charms. Like going barefoot, messing about in boats is a powerful instinctive pleasure for some of us. Who among us hasn't mused about retiring on a houseboat? Who stands gawking at a busy highway the way we gawk at a river full of boats? Who walks around a parking lot reading license plates as absorbed and happy as we walk around a marina reading the names of boats — *Ellen Sue, I'm Retired, Rover III, Crackerjack, Spindrift?* (Boats, large and small, have names. Pullman cars had names. Planes have only numbers.)

The sailboat slices silently through water while you're holding the wind itself in a big canvas pocket, two elements mastered at once. The canoe responds to your arms like a dancer. The motor-boat, or stinkpot, despised by sailors, is raw power at its finest, roaring and banging from wave-top to wave-top and annoying the fishermen. (The pleasure of irritating our fellow man, as in carrying loud music through the streets, is not one of our more adult traits, but it's undeniable.)

Dried sections of American canals are kept up only as educational relics, with a Park Service interpreter to explain them and perhaps a bike path where once the mules trod, but elsewhere they're liquid playgrounds. The governments of both England and France maintain at great expense and purely for pleasure the canal networks that were once industrial transportation. A Brit can live on his boat in the heart of London and then, when a gentle wanderlust strikes, putter all the way up to the Yorkshire Dales with side trips to Oxford and Wales, admiring the countryside at an un-American six kilometers an hour and tying up to refresh himself at canal-side pubs. Time-wasting at its finest.

Step into even the humblest rowboat and you can feel the gelatinous give and shift underfoot. The thin solid over thick liquid. The floor planking could be the soles of your feet; you're standing on water. Cast off into almost birdlike freedom; you needn't go where the road takes you, you can go wherever there's water. Turn left or right or in circles on its surface.

What's down underneath you feels alive. Flexible. Sometimes threatening. You've left the immovable land and gone back to the shifty old mother that bore you, and it pleases something deep in the tissues of the flesh.

For some. For those others who feel that boats, like bare feet, are not a sensuous pleasure but only an obsolete mode of travel, it's hard to explain.

Air

APPARENTLY the joy of breathing was once pretty readily available. At least, in the older novels and plays a character will say, "I'm going out for some fresh air," and simply step outside, without even his car keys. I don't see how this could have been true during the coal-burning years, and the poor folk in factory towns must have had trouble even recognizing each other through the air, let alone inhaling it. Still, "fresh air" was once a phrase in common use, and all it meant was outdoors. As recently as my own youth, children were chased out to play in it, and people religiously slept with the bedroom window open to let the stuff come in.

Now we're advised that outside is even deadlier than in. Our homes are infested with radon gas and a poison emitted by plastic as it ages and microscopic wriggly things that thrive in the dust under the bed, but outside is sudden death. Experts measure and report on it daily. "Air quality," they call it, and by "quality" they mean the invisible bulk of carcinogens, allergens, irritants, gas fumes, and evil spirits packed into the neighborhood today. They don't seem to have measurements for its good angels, positive measurements, for whatever makes the air, at some times, in some places, an active pleasure to breathe. "Air quality: Good" only means less grit, less poison, and I suppose there aren't even names for its various happy components that sometimes make us, even in cities, smile for no reason.

It's recognized that some airs are better, by which we mean cleaner, than others; the Fresh Air Fund wasn't established to round up farm boys and bus them to the South Bronx for the summer. But there's more to air than cleanliness or the smells it carries.

Of course, some of it's done with mere moisture content. After the cold, dry air of winter the spring damp tastes sweet, and after the humid languors of August, the first fall dryness lightens our steps. It's more complicated than that, though. There are secret ingredients. Transcendental pheromones that sneak in and smack us in the receptors.

At the moment I live on a mountain. Not much of a mountain by some standards, but high enough so that my eyes itch and turn red when I spend the night in a lowland town. Mountain air has always been considered more refined, its ingredients more *distillé*. I don't know whether official scientists recognize anything special about it now, or have a word for its wonders, but once they held it the only certain cure for tuberculosis and sent generations of patients uphill to lie around breathing it. Growers of mountain coffee advertise its origins. Natives of the high Andes are reputed to live more or less forever.

My own guests arrive, step out of the car, and cry "Smell that air!" I sniff obediently, and smell only that their car has been seriously taxed by the climb. Except in honeysuckle season it doesn't particularly smell, and what they mean is "Breathe that air!" It's a superior element. It elevates the spirit. Sound travels effortlessly through it. Then it puts the unacclimated guests to sleep at ten. "It's the air," they apologize, stumbling off to bed, where they sleep like rocks. Stimulant and narcotic combined, it's well worth breathing.

Other airs have other components. Sea air as an all-purpose medicine once had its adherents; mountains for the consumptive, but ships and shores for the neurasthenic and those whose health, in the ominous nineteenth-century phrase, was "broken." Unfortunately doctors, perhaps embarrassed by their ignorance of its nature, no longer recommend it, but we go anyway. We stand on deck or beach and face the water. If asked, we say we're looking at it, but it's usually rather monotonous to look at, and what we're doing is breathing its air, because it makes us feel good.

Forests have their own air. Maybe not the paltry Eastern woodlot, though pine woods brew a fine spicy compound, but the great, dimly lit, mossy forests of the Northwest. Here we draw pre-Columbian angels into the lungs and marvel bemusedly, feel vaguely religious, nonspecifically inspired. We might say we're impressed by the sheer size of the trees, but fully half our wondering comes through the air, which is unlike other airs, almost palpably pure, and spreads its spirits through the bloodstream and leaves us mysteriously pleased with life for days afterward, with a tendency to walk into the furniture.

The connoisseur of fresh air no longer steps outside to breathe it, even in the suburbs. Too many cars, trucks, furnaces, barbecue pits, and lawn mowers have been using it. He has to get in his own car now and drive away, spewing a trail of exhaust, to find a good breathing place. Park, walk away from his fuming vehicle, and stop to draw in long gulps of the real thing. "Smell that air," he says to his companions, and everyone takes a deep breath and smiles.

Fire

PPARENTLY the fire was caused by children playing with matches," says the television newsperson, and we all sigh and nod. Of course. We'd be surprised to hear that children were playing with, say, lentils, but everyone wants to play with matches. What possible toy could complete with the humble giveaway matchbook? Rub the cardboard stick on the black strip and look! *fire.*

The lightbulb is an efficient and useful invention, but lovers don't place it on the dinner table to hold hands around. At summer camp, we didn't sit in a circle around a flashlight singing "Row, Row, Row Your Boat" and "Taps." No church ever suggested sacrificing our firstborn to the lightbulb gods. Fire is powerful basic magic and we yearn toward it like a bunch of moths, lusting after something deeper than heat and light. Families don't gather in front of a radiator to crack nuts and tell stories, and fireplaces converted to the safer, cleaner gas flame are disguised as the real thing with a bundle of birch logs pretending to burn.

It goes way back. The ethnographers Sumner and Keller say, "Man is scarcely man till he is in possession of fire." Before we learned to capture and feed it, and later make it from — literally — scratch, we were the least of beings. Furless and naked, we had to huddle together in the hottest climates. Sometimes other, better-equipped animals ate us in our sleep, and if we managed to eat them first they were raw, and this was no corn-fed steak tartare either.

Then some smart ancestor got a piece of the stuff and learned how to keep it alive — or, if you insist, Prometheus brought some back from the sun — and suddenly we were in charge. We could chase away the tigers and drive the more edible creatures out into plain sight by burning the brush, and kill them with fire-sharpened sticks, and barbecue them into chewability. We could move on to colonize the cooler climates, relieving population pressure in the Olduvai Gorge, and if our neighbors got on our nerves anyway we could burn their huts down around their ears.

Fire, the first taste of power. We looked upon ourselves and found us good. We were boss. Probably, we decided, we also had minds and souls; probably we were in a whole different category from the other animals; probably we were unique. If, as is currently held, self-esteem is the key to success, we were on our way.

Now, in a city apartment, the treasured wood-burning fireplace adds thousands to the rent, but we want it anyway. We stop at the neighborhood convenience store and buy three sticks of wood strapped together, pay dearly for them, and carry them home in triumph. Their thump and clatter on the hearth sounds the same as it has for untold thousands of years. "I thought we could have a fire tonight," we say, with a kind of shy pride, as if we had brought pearls and rubies. We crumple newspapers and strike a match while the family gathers to watch.

We sit for an hour staring at it. Something inside us was hungry for this, for the color and movement of flame. Long, slow waves of prehistoric satisfaction roll in from the farthest shores of the past and wash through our blood.

The most frequently mentioned goals in the "Personals" ads are fireside evenings and dinners by candlelight; fire supervising both the flames of passion and the warm glow of domesticity, where the hearth is the heart of home.

Fire, centerpiece of civilization, with Rome's vestal virgins tending the sacred flame that must never go out; the Greek Olympic torch handed from runner to runner.

It's a purely psychic pleasure now that we don't really need its light and warmth. (When Richard Nixon was in the White House he liked a good fire in the fireplace even in Washington's August, and had to keep the air conditioners raging at full blast to stand it.)

If we just wanted to watch something moving we could turn on a television basketball game. We want fire for its own sake. We want it in spite of lightbulbs and central heating.

On a cold, dark, misty day we feel an almost physical urge to build a fire no matter how warm and bright our homes are, because some of our pleasures have roots too deep to argue with. We want to play with matches; it's important. Don't ask.

Water

WHERE I live, the quality of water is a subject for connoisseurs rather than chemists. The old-timers know my aquifer and nod approvingly: Best water on the mountain, they say. Water, plain water, un-bottled, domestic, is still a recognized drink here; outside workmen come to the kitchen door and ask for it by name. Coffee, Coke, and beer are refused politely. They drink and hand me back the glass. "Good water," they say, and I'm flattered, as if I'd personally made it and poured it into the well.

Visitors from the city drink themselves bloated and carry it home in jugs, since few drink city water for pleasure now, and perhaps they shouldn't. Once we were told to drink, for our health's sake, eight full glasses of it a day, but I haven't heard anyone mention it lately. From time to time bulletins are issued, reassuring the public that the funny smell means nothing; ignore it. Then other bulletins appear telling us not to worry about something called THM; it's an unavoidable result of all the chlorine they add to keep us from getting cholera, and besides, it doesn't give *everyone* cancer, and anyway which would you rather, cancer or cholera?

When I get older and more crotchety I'll start carrying a flask of my well water when visiting in cities, and use it to dampen my toothbrush.

It's a good well, and all year round it runs pure and inspiriting and cold — stingingly cold; a sudden soaking from the hose can cause heart attacks. And a good well is, so to speak, all very well, but it isn't the same as a spring.

Around here, all the best places have springs. All the old places. Few people now depend solely on them, on the bucket dippered up and carried sloshing to the kitchen to be set on the table while the silt and wriggly things settle, the way we did in the cabin down the hill when I was a bucket-lugging child. The springs are still here, though. They've been marking their tracts of land as buildings sites since time and the hill began.

At Skyfields, half a mile to the north, there's one known locally as Washington's Spring. They say that George, surveying for the Fairfaxes in these parts, often made the steep side trip up from the Gap for its water, because it was famous water. Better than other waters. A hundred years later Mosby's Rangers were grateful for it as they lurked up here waiting to knock off the Yankee wagon trains passing over the Gap. Unlike the puddle down at the cabin, Washington's Spring lives in its own stone receptacle, or altar, roofed to keep out the leaves. Its runoff once traveled in a mossy trench through the springhouse to cool the butter and milk that lolled there in Mason jars. In July, a sweaty child could push open the heavy, insulating door and go in and crouch in the chilly dark, shivering gratefully.

Springs shaped the country. For the Indians, the distance from spring to spring dictated where the trails went. Then for the traveler and his horse, following the Indian trails, the spring was a necessary refreshment stop, sometimes a place to meet up with other travelers and exchange the news.

For the settler, the spring meant "Live here." It meant, "Build a house; drink; wash; water your horses and your vegetable patch; keep your milk from souring. Live and be welcome."

The settler had sense enough not to send a sample of the water to the state for analysis. Probably it contained its quota of coliform bacteria. Indeed, it may be that E. *coli* is everywhere, in the air, in the yogurt. It may even be good for us. Maybe all that supersanitized water full of carcinogenic THMs is so clean it kills off essential creatures in the intestinal tract as well as possibly nonessential ones in the reservoirs and causes the whole country to suffer from stone bowels, known on television as "occasional irregularity." Maybe we *need* a good dose of E. *coli*.

Before the invention of water analysis, towns grew up and prospered around a generous spring. The East is dotted with places named Springfield, Springhouse, Berkeley Springs, Cold Springs, Warm Springs, Sinking Springs, Spring City.

Maybe, if we were a more gracious, less bossy and meddling species, we'd have made our homes only where the earth said we could. We didn't, though. We pushed in everywhere, drilling. My family was never invited to build this house. In order to live here we had to dig a well.

A well is an invasion, almost a theft. Men had to drag in heavy machinery and pierce the earth's skin and drill into its flesh until they struck water; I suck it out of the land with a pump, against its will. Oh, it's the same water as Washington's, but it feels man-made rather than magic.

A spring is a gift. It lies on the top of the land waiting to be scooped up in a bent tin cup or with the bare hands. It offers itself freely to bird, beast, and insect as well as man; at the cabin, raccoons roiled and muddied it hunting for crayfish, and sometimes, in a dry season, a thirsty copperhead and I surprised each other.

Creek water or river water was always a crapshoot, even in cleaner days. Exposed on the surface of the world, it carried whatever trickled into it upstream, or whatever tripped and fell heavily into it, drowned, and rotted. Spring water, sealed in the dark mysteries out of sight, was clean. It was primevally pure, pure as the world on the third day of creation.

In the old world lots of springs are holy, for one reason or another. Water was always a lightning rod for holiness: baptism, and the Ganges, and the sprinkle of blessed water in the corners of a new house that drives out evil spirits. Holiness that would blow away in the air or get plowed under in the earth can live in springwater for millennia. People made pilgrimages and carried water home in little bottles, just as city shoppers today carry little bottles of Perrier or Pelegrino tenderly home to serve with dinner instead of wine.

Springwater has particularly mystic powers. Legions of invalids have trooped to Saratoga Springs, White Sulphur Springs, Yellow Springs, Hot Springs, all the curative spas where they lay around in the waters and drank them by the gallon and felt miraculously better. Powerful juju, springwater.

You can't buy a spring. You can't make a spring where no spring was before. In folk and Biblical stories springs bubble suddenly forth to mark the sites of miracles, martyrdoms, apparitions, and cataclysms. Any old mortal can dig a well, but springwater calls for a special event.

You can tell by the first taste.

Speed

P
ROBABLY it's a sign of psychological health to like speed; it shows self-confidence and that absence of imagination that's such a factor in sanity and self-confidence. Self-confident dogs like it too. Given half a chance, a dog will run as if pursued by dragons toward no particular goal, or even around in circles. He'll hang perilously out of the car window to feel the wind whipping his ears and blowing his eyes shut. (Cats, who may have more imagination or better sense, hide under the seat and moan warnings of impending doom.)

Speed haunts our metaphors: the front-runner, the fast lane, the finish line, the mayoral race. Faster is better and the race is, usually, to the swift, just as the battle is to the strong, whatever Ecclesiastes told you. Besides, it's fun.

We must have come naturally to this taste. We're a slow species; we can't even outrun a chipmunk, much less a tiger, and I expect this griped us from the beginning. Long ago, stumbling and gasping, we gave up and watched dinner hightailing it effortlessly over the hill, or glanced over our shoulder at the bear that was effortlessly gaining on us, and surely it was reasonable to want to be faster. If we were going to get anywhere at all or catch anything to eat, it was clear we couldn't do it on our personal feet like everything else.

At some point, isolated genius-humans — who seem to have been responsible for everything that gets done around here — realized that if we stopped eating horses and climbed up on them instead, letting the horse's feet do the walking, we'd arrive at our destinations sooner. (Similar discoveries were made with camels and elephants. One can only speculate about the failed experiments with, say, wild boars, pythons, ostriches, etc.) The horse was an instant hit. Civilizations on horseback rode roughshod over those on foot. All those equestrian statues that decorate our public squares testify that the man on a horse was a hero, the man afoot left far behind in the dust and dung.

Dizzy with success, we went on to invent a lot of hardware — the wheel, the saddle and bridle, chariots, planes, dogsleds, elephant howdahs, Harley-Davidsons, rollerblades, trolley cars. We had to get fast the hard way, but here we finally are, and we love it.

For fullest enjoyment, we have to be out there in it, or in charge of it. The only point of the Concorde — besides showing how rich and busy you are — is to arrive in Paris earlier. It doesn't *feel* fast, not fast like thirty miles an hour on skis or a bobsled or a sailboat. The more insulated we are from the wind of our passage the faster we have to go to feel fast. This is the purpose of convertibles: with the top down we can stay within the speed limit and still get our cheeks reddened and our hair tangled by speed. In a big, closed, comfortable car, even seventy feels like strolling.

Some of us — men in particular; testosterone is a factor — drive twenty miles out of our way to find a fast highway to travel on rather than the closer, shorter, two-lane road. Speed is what the car is all about, what it's made for. We find it enraging to dawdle in traffic punctuated by red lights; dawdling, our car is but a caged and flightless bird and so are we.

Our speeding tickets are a kind of trophy collection, bagged through our personal valor, our swiftness in the great race of life, and those who have never been pulled over by staties admire them enviously, feeling like the poor, spiritless, plodding wimps that they are.

The joy of speed in a car is confused a bit by the engine's association with power — which is fun too, but different. Purer forms of speed are unmotorized and unconnected with testosterone, as in windsurfing or coasting down long hills on a bike; all we need do is hang on. At the amusement park we can sit on a square of carpet and rocket down the great slide with the wind in our ears and the scenery rushing up to meet us; satisfying but childish. As we get older our lust for speed is more and more channeled into the car and the foot on the gas.

Speed to a cheetah may be all in the day's work, but for us heavy-footed clods it lifts up the heart. It calls to us in clarion tones and elevates us to the status of at least the rabbit, if not the noble horse. The wind sings success in our ears. Billboards zip by too fast to read. Like Mr. Toad, we cry, "The motor-car went Poop-poop-poop / As it raced along the road," and we head for the level stretch where we can really open her up and see what she can do. We are, after all, the cleverest of all species, and now we're the fastest too. No wonder it makes us happy.

Of course this doesn't explain why dogs like speed; they were always fast enough on their feet. Maybe I'm wrong and there's a simpler, more universal element involved for both of us. Maybe even cheetahs love it for its own sake and not just for the breakfast it brings; maybe they run races with friends in order to feel the wind in their ears. Maybe fast is simply a basic form of physical entertainment, like a kind of sanitized sex — for all but the faint of heart and the cat under the front seat howling doomsday.

Driving Beltless

B ACK before seat belts were, first, available and then later compulsory, we didn't count driving without them as one of life's joys; it was merely a basic civil right, like breathing or voting. Now being able to wiggle, reach, bend, stretch, or change position in the driver's seat is a criminal act, punishable by fines varying in ferocity from state to state, and takes its place with Eve's apple among the heady stolen pleasures.

I am a virtuous citizen and easily intimidated, and I buckle my seat belt more or less automatically. They keep telling me it will save my life, and I keep trying to believe them, though what I drive looks less like a car than a roller-skate and would offer about as much protection in a crash. I cling to a vision of the whole flimsy structure demolished by a truck, its fragments flung to the winds and fluttering down the median strip like discarded McDonald's boxes, and only my belted self in the driver's seat still intact, perched bemused but upright on the roadbed. At least this is the way I understand the official scenario, and I suppose, rather sourly, that traveling in harness is a small price to pay for survival. I suppose it's sweet that the government cares so for my well-being that they've made it illegal for me to risk it.

Once or twice a month, though, I drive a few country miles unstrapped. Not too often, because I'd hate to blunt the thrill. Grinning guiltily, glancing around for sheriff's cars, I soar down the long hill from the Gap, me and my little scrap of a car, free and equal, light and lithe, neither of us lashed to the other. I shift in my seat, confirming my liberty. I bend. I sway. I have sawed through the bars, tunneled under the moat, escaped with Pegasus himself between my knees, treading clouds.

When we get to Round Hill I'll restrap the leash, but in the meantime it's very sweet, and all the sweeter for being against the law. No wonder our ancestors drank so much gin in the twenties.

Whistling

ANYONE Can Whistle," according to Stephen Sondheim, but I never could. As a child I wanted to, desperately. I thought if I could whistle it would spread open and light up my whole life and make me a different person. I thought it would be my best and bravest companion. I thought nobody who could whistle would ever be completely unhappy or very badly frightened, and I was probably right on all points.

I was the wrong sex. Boys whistled. It may actually be a sex-linked talent; certainly society wanted it to be. As grandmothers used to say,

> A whistling girl and a crowing hen
> Both will come to a bad end.

Those birdlike sounds stand for all that's cocky, breezy, capable, independent, in-your-face — in short, everything dangerously ungirlish. Having achieved only a single, breathy, wavering peep, I resigned myself to listening.

People used to whistle in the streets. Singing in the streets is usually taken as a sign of drunkenness or mental imbalance and can lead to arrest, but whistling was always proper. It seemed to go well with walking, though never with jogging, of course. Messenger boys whistled. It's a traveler's sound. Jan Morris, footloose adventurer and poker into strange corners of the earth, admits to being a street-whistler still, but they're an endangered breed.

Apparently electronics wiped it out, and those who like a tune to lighten their steps plug into earphones and a pocket tape-player, in keeping with the new wisdom that music of any kind is best left to professionals. It's a loss. A stray scrap of whistle perked up the day, and at night, an invisible stranger piping a cheerful "Clementine" or a poignant "Greensleeves" made the dark a lot friendlier.

To whistle while you work, like Snow White's seven dwarfs, means pleasure in the task, competence, and a certain anarchy; you're working because you choose to, and you'll take no bullying from the boss. For two cents you'd stick your thumbs in your pockets and saunter off the job. Whistling.

For years I went to a whistling dentist, and lay back relaxed under his hands: here was a happy man who enjoyed his work and had every confidence in his own skill; a man who had never excavated the wrong tooth or slipped a drill through the customer's jaw. The whistle said it all.

A two-note or sliding whistle is a universal summons. It's traditional for dogs, and even the unsummonable cat throws the whistler an alert, questioning look; unlike mere singing, whistling is a trans-species message. "Whistle, and she'll come to you," said Beaumont and Fletcher in the early 1600s. "Oh whistle, and I'll come to ye, my lad," sang Robert Burns. "You know how to whistle, don't you?" said Bacall to Bogart. "Give a little whistle," said Jiminy Cricket to Pinocchio. Falconers whistle for their falcons and shepherds for their sheep. In the theater, to whistle backstage summons bad luck. On ships, sailors whistled for a breeze. All sorts of things come when whistled for.

Courage, for instance. "Whistling to keep myself from being afraid," wrote John Dryden in the seventeenth century, echoed in the twentieth in *The King and I* with "Whistle a Happy Tune." Whistling in the dark, we call it. It's the very sound of courage; courage hears it and comes running.

To walk away whistling is the pinnacle of carefree independence.

The whistler never looks back, regrets nothing, apologizes for nothing, and may never stop walking till he comes to the sea.

I was right; everything would have worked out differently if only I'd been able to learn. Falcons would have dropped from the sky to my wrist.

At least for years I could listen and take heart vicariously, but now it's fading from the streets. I can't hear even a ten-year-old boy whistling up his dog. Have we forgotten how? The nonwhistler can't imagine why anyone with such a joyful talent would stifle it. I hope the Sony Walkman is really the only culprit. I hope it doesn't mean that people have lost not the knack but the impulse; that the jaunty whistling *feeling* I longed for has somehow leaked out of our lives.

I wonder if Australians whistle.

Fall

IN the olden days, and maybe still in some places, the living-room furniture was dressed for summer in "slipcovers" — flowered chintz, as I remember, light in color, cool under the bare legs, lush with cabbage roses and vine leaves. In the fall these were taken off, washed, hung on the line to billow in the chilly sunshine, and then put away in chests. The scratchy wool or prickly plush upholstery was revealed, plum-colored or brown or forest green so as not to show dirt because, unlike the slipcovers, it couldn't be laundered and hung on the line. Grass matting was rolled up and stored and the serious rugs of winter came out of mothballs. Life is real, life is earnest, dark, harsh to the touch, businesslike, enduring, and sober — we'd known all along that summer was just a mask. A lightweight, flowered veneer.

The only thing really wrong with fall is that it means summer's over and winter's coming. For people over forty, this is a metaphor for the passing of youth and the approach of doddering, a prospect that few really relish. As the Bard so gloomily puts it,

> For never-resting time leads summer on
> To hideous winter and confounds him there;
> Sap checked with frost and lusty leaves quite gone,
> Beauty o'ersnow'd and bareness every where.

It's hard to cherish a season for its own sake when it smells like the darkening passageway to death.

Those under forty suffer from unsettling waves of anxiety and elation as they alternately expect someone to send them back to school and then realize that no one can.

For some of us, myself included, our winter selves seem so radically different from our summer selves that the transition — the taking-off of summer's slouching, vaporous languors and the buttoning-on of winter — can be a clumsy struggle and stresses the immune system. Great numbers of us come down with minor diseases in the early fall, either because we dread the coming darkness and its ominous winds, or because we think if we get sick enough they won't make us go to school.

In all these matters, fall is an innocent bystander, a harmless messenger. In many areas fall is far nicer than spring, and in some years the season of mists and mellow fruitfulness lingers for long, warm weeks, illuminated by the torches of maples on the hill and goldenrod in the ditches. Legions of drivers make horrid the byways of Vermont to stare at leaves, storing up color against the dark to come.

Spring is almost always tardy, at least to our minds, and disappointing, and muddy underfoot, and punctuated by surprise snows that bury the daffodil and frosts that blast the peach blossom. Every day of spring is a delay on the road to glorious summer; every day of fall is a delay on the road to hideous winter.

In America the season pivots on Labor Day, which has been mistakenly placed too early on the calendar, weeks before official fall. After Labor Day life takes its annual turn for the serious and the ambitious make resolutions: to stop smoking, enroll in night classes, work out in a gym. (The reason so many New Year's resolutions get forgotten is that the new calendar year begins in the dark heart of winter, with nothing to mark it but the date on our checks. Nothing is changed; spring is still far away, and the coat we wear is the coat we were wearing before, so the occasion seems too contrived and artificial to warrant a new life and kinder, healthier habits. Labor Day, on the other hand, is fraught with meaning.)

The air lightens, the sweat dries, footsteps quicken, shadows have sharp edges, and people with pollen allergies start praying for frost. Those of us with slipcovers can take them off and wash them. Country folk can get in their winter's wood, making busy and cheerful the autumn weekends with the growl of chainsaw and the bark of mallet on splitting-wedge. This is pleasurable because it brings the premature satisfaction of triumph over the elements: let winter come; with the strength of our own backs and hands we have defended our home from freezing. City folk can buy new clothes, solemn clothes to signify renewed industry, and put away the bathing suits, the frivolous linens and pastels of childish summer. Shake out and press the stored wool suits. This is pleasurable because it means we are, once again, adults to be listened to and reckoned with.

Even our dinner turns a seasonal corner as soon as the last tomato vine is yanked from the ground and dumped in cellar or garage, perhaps to ripen a few more fruits in the protected darkness while the outside garden blackens under frost. We turn our appetite to meat again, and simmered sauces, and roasted carrots, onions, and potatoes, those sturdy underground staples that satisfy the inner primitive because they've seen our kind through centuries of winters: with roots enough in the root-cellar we shall not starve before asparagus comes round again.

No matter how civilized we are, we prepare for winter; stock up, like squirrels, thicken our fur and brace ourselves, because that's what creatures do in the so-called temperate zone. We clean out the roof gutters and check the antifreeze, and our busyness kindles the warm glow of competence. Prepared, we even look forward to the worst of weathers and feel mildly let down by unseasonable warm spells.

Some of us pass our days completely separated from the weather; our homes and offices are cooled or heated; at workday's end we proceed to our cooled or heated car by elevator or underground passage, drive home and into our garages. Protecting us from the ancient realities of heat and cold, this also cuts us off from the satisfactions of the season and the stately progress of the year. Only our clocks and calendars tell us what time it is, when to take off the slipcovers and when to put them on.

Of course, there are places where fall never comes. Places with only a rainy season and a dry season, or a tourist season and a cut-rate season. People who live there never put these clothes away and take out those clothes, or remove the flowered slipcovers to expose the prickly brown reality of life. Like butterflies, they do not chop wood, neither do they put up storm-windows; they just go on dancing and singing all year round.

The rest of us are free to sneer at the childish fantasy of their lives. We can even pity them a bit, because their pleasure in a pretty day is so faint and threadbare compared with the surprised freshness of our own.

This is a consolation, if a small one, for the chilblains and tire chains to come.

Gambling

TACITUS noticed that the Germanic tribes, even when cold sober, would gamble themselves into slavery. In China, a dedicated gambler might wager his own right hand, though it's hard to know what use this was to the winner. Emperors Augustus and Nero set up state lotteries to fatten the national treasury; so did Queen Elizabeth I. In America, snobs who wouldn't be seen dead with a lottery ticket play the stock market.

We like to gamble. Winning, we have closed our eyes, leapt across the yawning abyss, and landed knee-deep in daisies. Even losing has a certain gloomy glamour: the gods of chance are worthy opponents; we have engaged them in hand-to-hand combat and though we lost, at least we shrank not from the contest.

Naturally the higher the stakes the more exciting it gets, and some hold that it can't be called gambling at all if we can afford to lose. Risk — the depth of the abyss — is the champagne of the bloodstream. The thrill is also deepened when, instead of merely checking numbers in the paper, we have a personal, hands-on relationship with the matter; kiss and throw the dice ourselves, or howl as our horse drops behind in the backstretch. Buying more lottery tickets than we can afford simply doesn't provide the same quickening of the pulse, not like slapping the deed to the house on the table among the chips and drawing to a busted flush. It helps to be there.

People have so much fun gambling that for generations most forms of it were illegal in most of the United States. The Puritans considered it blasphemous, and later churches railed against its wickedness except when church-sponsored, as in Wednesday-night Bingo games to benefit the new social hall. The upper and lower classes continued to gamble anyway. It seems to be basic to the human animal. When I was in elementary school, little boys pitched pennies in dark corners of the playground; the attendant penalties were awful to contemplate and must surely have added to the fun.

Illegality reinforced the joy of gambling and produced colorful *Guys and Dolls* characters and a steady income for the Mafia, while many an underpaid policeman sent his kids to college on the bribes. Then in 1951 the Kefauver Committee did a little snooping and announced that illegal gambling around here came to $20 billion a year, and in 1951 that wasn't chump-change. The government, nobody's fool, realized they weren't getting any of this, so they made the gamblers sign up to pay taxes.

Little by little, respectability has reared its ugly head. This is due to the link between taxes and morality, by which everything that produces taxable income is fine with us; losing your shirt at Las Vegas or Pimlico is unfortunate but morally okay; losing it at the Saturday-night poker game is wicked, because the winners won't be telling the IRS.

Some complain that gambling is now so respectable it's quite dismally middle class and much of the joy has fled, what with everyone and his dog playing the slots and lotteries, and no office without its football pool. Gone are the fleet and skulking numbers runners; gone the sinister hats and snappy suits of the Damon Runyon touts; gone even the dazzlingly wicked concept of vingt-et-un at Monte Carlo, where countesses in shoulder-length black gloves wagered their diamond earrings and Russian Grand Dukes, having lost an estate the size of Nebraska, shot themselves on balconies. What, alas, do we need with Monte Carlo when Atlantic City's so much closer, and has saltwater taffy besides?

Fiddlesticks. This is like saying the sexual revolution of the sixties took all the fun out of sex. What gambling has lost in romance it's gained in availability, and it is our duty in these pages to provide pleasure for all, even the respectable. Elitists who still miss the illicit thrill can always try Russian roulette.

Scenery

I N days gone by, when people wanted to look at a nice piece of landscape they got in the car on a Sunday afternoon and drove out to where the fields and cows began. Now the suburbs and industrial parks stretch to the horizon and the driver figures he might as well just keep going till he gets to Yellowstone.

The uglier and more cramped we make our immediate territory, the more we yearn for something satisfying to look at, quite possibly something that looks just like our own neighborhood thirty years ago. Every summer millions of us hit the road in search of handsome views, meadows, lakes, mountains, autumn foliage. Scenery. Distance. Space.

The eyes' lust for long views may date from our roots back on the savannah, where we hoisted ourselves up on our hind legs to peer over the tops of the grasses: the farther we could see, the better. Short views were usually hiding disagreeable surprises with sharp teeth. Now that we're more sophisticated and less worried about predators, we'd be bored by flat grass clear to the horizon. We like a bit of visual entertainment; a hill, a lone pine tree, a river, some tastefully arranged clouds. A ship, a lighthouse.

Some fierce purists insist on total wilderness, without so much as the sniff of another human's campfire on the breeze, but most of us like the suggestion of a human touch. A red barn, a church steeple, a winding road. Things that people made. They're reassuring. What Sir Francis Bacon or somebody called "homo aditus naturae," or Friday's footprint, reminding us that we haven't been left all alone here with nothing but God and geology. (I suppose this accounts for the success of curiosities like Mount Rushmore, the wilderness decorated and humanized by Teddy Roosevelt's eyeglasses carved in majestic granite.)

As Barry Lopez said in *Arctic Dreams*, "Traces of human presence in the land, like maps, organize undifferentiated space in certain ways, and the effect, especially in open country, is soothing." Of course, being snobs, we draw the line at the carcass of a Studebaker against a backdrop of bottles and bedsprings. We like high-class human traces. Something agricultural, for choice, because part of us still buys into the pipe dreams of Wordsworth and Jefferson, and delights to muse on how nobly picturesque the simple farmer is compared with, say, the simple stockbroker.

The human touch on scenery is one of the reasons we keep going to Europe, a human-friendly landscape brought to heel uncounted generations ago. The roads were laid down by Romans, the forests lie open like parks, the many-bridged rivers are kindly to boats, the hills sloping down to the bay are layered with pretty houses, and the elegant, straight rows of trees along the road were planted by human hands. We know our own wild country is grander, and we drive long distances to appreciate it — the Black Hills, Death Valley, the bayous, the Maine woods, the Everglades, the Great Lakes — but it's lonely out there and just possibly haunted; we didn't come honestly by these spaces and our racial conscience sits a bit uneasily.

A good-looking piece of scenery anywhere delights the eye and elevates the spirits. Some of us, crude creatures that we are, are merely excited; finer souls draw ethical and spiritual nutrients from the sight. (Either way, this is one of life's late-blooming tastes, like naps, and parents needn't bother driving small children around to see the purple mountains' majesties; the children will go right on duking it out in the back seat and whining for food as if you were showing them Cincinnati. No one under twenty really wants to look at scenery.)

From where I sit at the moment, I can see the last narrow V of what was once, before the trees grew, a valley-wide view, friendly with miniature farms and orchards and a ribbon of road that twinkled at night. The place felt different, back when you could see so far. Being here felt aloof, powerful, Olympian. Looking down across all that space was like flying. Now, except for the last sliver between the trees, the house feels more like a house in the woods than a house on a hill, and the difference is noticeable in every room, a humbling difference, a basic difference that penetrates everything done and said here and even alters the dreams of overnight guests.

I'm going to get the trees cut. It will be staggeringly expensive, but it's important. The house was built up here under the same compulsion that has sent people climbing up on things since time began: to look out over the scenery below. Without its view the house will suffocate. I must cut the trees and blast a tracheotomy out to the view, so the place can breathe some scenery again.

The indigenous Indians here burned the woods down on a regular basis so they, too, could see farther. See what was coming, friend or foe, sunshine or thunderstorm. They refused to live or even go hunting in places without a good, long, satisfying view. I understand perfectly.

Bad Words

WE ought to get up a committee to protest the increasing use of obscene language in movies and on radio and cable television. This is a wholly deplorable trend, blunting the ordinary civilian's illicit joy in using these words himself. Once, when broadcasters let slip a naughty expression, they were instantly banished from the airwaves and had to do public penance before their voices could be heard again. Now they're positively encouraged, and some have built substantial followings using no other discernible talent. If bad words continue to be flung about so freely, the thrill will fade.

Wherever he went, the late, great Lenny Bruce gave the local police a chance to hang around nightclubs and catch the show for free. They were on duty, waiting to arrest him for saying bad words.

Arrests and subsequent trials gave him fresh material, as in the famous "Blah-blah-blah" case. Blah-blah-blah, he explained in a later, sanitized routine, is a ten-letter word beginning with "c" and signifying the performer of a certain act of oral sex; for using the word itself he was arrested and stood trial. At the trial, everyone involved was explicit about the offense. Explicit over and over and over.

The arresting officer and the judge made sure they understood each other: "Your honor, he said blah-blah-blah." "He said blah-blah-blah?" "Up on the stage, in front of women and a mixed audience, he said blah-blah-blah." "He said blah-blah-blah?" "Then," says Bruce, "I dug something; they sort of *liked* saying blah-blah-blah. Because they said it a few extra times. . . . The bailiff is yelling, 'What did he say?' 'Shut up, you blah-blah-blah!' . . . '*Goddamn*! it's *good* to say blah-blah-blah!' "

It *is* fun. Cussing is a great releaser of the tensions, a detumescence, a loosening of the corsets and lightening of the accumulated load, a stimulating explosion in the cylinder head of the spirit. Like so many joys, bad words suffer dilution from overuse, and those who have served in the armed forces, advertising agencies, or the Nixon White House may find they have lost their savor and deliver no more thrill than crying "Confusion!" or "Seattle!" For fullest enjoyment they should be used sparingly, by those raised in households where children had their mouths washed out with soap and gathered later, in secret, to share their latest four-letter acquisitions. For such, even an occasional "damn it" becomes a badge of freedom and mark of maturity, like the well-chilled martini, and continues to give satisfaction for many years.

There are nuances of difference between blasphemy and obscenity. Obscenity is fun for all, but blasphemy delivers its purest pleasure to the devout; notice how Catholics are forever telling salacious jokes about nuns and priests, which leave the rest of the world bored blue. The more constricted the user, the greater the release. At their most deeply enjoyable, bad words must be felt to be bad indeed, to be agents of evil, launched into the air by irresponsible tongues and armed with unimaginable secret weapons. Oddly, these airborne enemies are effective only when used in their pristine form. Words that merely represent bad words, like "darn" for damn or "shoot" for shit, completely hoodwink the powers of darkness and are never evil and consequently never much fun.

They can also sound rather silly. When President Bush flew into a rage and thundered to the world that Saddam Hussein was making him mad as heck, some citizens admired the virtuous euphemism — him being an ex-Navy man who probably knew different words — while others thought he sounded like somebody's grandmother who'd dropped a stitch in her knitting. Strong troubles call for strong language.

Ethnic slurs are excepted, of course, but these aren't usually delivered for pleasure and don't usually produce it. WASPs raised in socially correct households find it hard to enjoy muttering "kike" or "nigger"; some guilts have burrowed too deep and undermine the thrill of sin. We've all heard our friends speak uncharitably, even viciously, of various groups of folk without ever uttering the wrong words. Perhaps they're restrained by the sense that racial epithets aren't just bad, they're lower-class. Trashy, low-rent, trailer-park words, akin to sloppy grammar.

To return to the authority, Lenny Bruce, in one of his more affecting routines, advocated widespread use of the word "nigger." He wanted all of us to use it at all times, in all contexts, until dailiness made it an ordinary, harmless arrangement of consonants and vowels like any other, and no little black kid would ever again come home from school crying because someone called him "nigger."

If ordinary use could rub the pain from "nigger," it could also rub the joy from "fuck."

Hostile epithets aside, bad language is a pure and harmless pleasure, the reckless smashing of a taboo without hurting a fly. For the strictly raised, even whispering it in private is enough to pack a punch; for those more casual, it helps to shock someone besides oneself.

According to legend, Zelda Fitzgerald found herself — the story doesn't say *how* — at a party full of intensely polite and respectable people. One of the suburban matrons rushed up to her and burbled that she, Zelda, must feel privileged to be helpmeet and inspiration to the great F. Scott. Pretty Zelda, sweetly demurring, smiled and said, "Oh, all I do is fuck."

The chances are she enjoyed this more fully than if she'd said the same thing in a Marine barracks. The joy of shocking, though perhaps childish, is not to be sneezed at. If no one is shocked, the fun's gone.

Bad language is one of our least expensive and most flexible pleasures, ready to hand wherever we may be. Unlike hot coffee, it requires no preparation; unlike champagne, it leaves no headache; unlike pets, it doesn't need to be fed and walked. It won't even make us fat or late for work. Enjoy — sparingly.

Winter

"IF Winter comes," asked Shelley, "can Spring be far behind?"

Yes.

Winter-lovers hold themselves morally superior to summer-lovers, and moral superiority is one of life's great joys. They look upon summer-lovers as timid, slothful, and probably helpless on skis or behind the wheel in freezing slush. They know we feel that subfreezing temperatures are hostile and out to get us, while the roadways want to murder us outright. They, gallant spirits, merrily embrace the challenges from which we shrink.

They are, to put it bluntly, a pain in the ass, but there's no denying they're having fun.

The winter-lover strides around the office, all but beating his or her chest, and cries, "I love the winter! I love cold weather! It makes me feel so *alive!*" Beyond the windows the rain segues into rattling sleet and then hushes to blobs of snow. Colleagues at the watercooler gulp vitamin C, cough, sniffle, and, in March, keep checking the calendar as one checks one's watch at a long meeting: Surely, surely, it must be the tenth or eleventh by now? Can it really be only the sixth? while the winter-lover struts and crows and broadcasts plans to weekend even farther north, where the snow is deeper and the lakes more stiffly frozen.

Now that the suntan of summer has gone the way of bacon and eggs, the skier's windburn and occasional crutches have replaced it as emblems of vigor and the healthy outdoor life. If the summer sun has become our enemy, dark winter must be our new friend. The brave leap into its arms. The rest of us can only wait for July, when the wretched creatures wilt, sweat, sicken, and turn pale. "I love the heat," we can say, blooming aggressively.

The trouble with winter is that it's winter all the way through. Other seasons make progress; temperatures grow warmer or cooler, waves of flowers or leaf colors succeed each other. Winter simply moves in and stops dead. The snows of December look remarkably like the snows of March, and a bare tree remains a bare tree for months. Only the contracting and then expanding hours of daylight show any sign of time passing. Small wonder our ancestors whooped it up at the solstice — how else to sustain our loony faith in spring, with nature in a coma or possibly stone-cold dead?

There are pleasures to be wrung from winter, though many are negative ones, like finally getting our feet warm or the car started or the walk cleared.

There's sex, for instance. It stands to reason that sex is better in winter than in summer; old-timers may remember Cole Porter's song, "Too Darn Hot," in *Kiss Me, Kate*. The healthy human body radiates a temperature of 98.6, or considerably warmer than the usual room, and winter urges us to cuddle up to it, as cats who sleep widely separated in August are inextricably entwined in January. Obstetricians are of fond of saying, "If we've had a bad winter, I'll have a busy fall."

Sex in front of an open fireplace (see FIRE) was more entertaining than sex in front of the ecologically correct sealed woodstove, but all is not lost; sex under a down comforter beats wrestling with the heaped blankets of yesteryear.

Then there are the winter projects. Winter is the natural time to clean out the files, read the great books of the Western world, build bookshelves, knit sweaters, and organize the basement. Completing these tasks gives us the glow of accomplishment plus the sense of time freed up for different pursuits in better weather.

A December sunset can be a fine sight, though the most vivid ones foretell the bitterest nights.

A couple of inches of new-fallen snow looks pretty, at least for a while, and covers up all that hideous bare ground and dead grass; April snow on green grass and crocuses isn't nearly as nice.

Deeper snow can mean all bets are off and all responsibilities on hold, at least until the plows get through.

Winter-lovers claim to enjoy the look of the world in winter, reduced to basics; the elaborate skeletons of trees, the stark contours of the land laid bare, and so forth. Others are reminded of nudist colonies, where the naked flesh is only sometimes more delightful than its discarded clothes.

Somehow even the heartiest snowbirds are rarely heard to exclaim, "I can't believe it's almost April. Where did the winter go?"

Wearing Fur

I FOUND it in the thrift shop, a rabbit-fur jacket of the most hauntingly subtle reddish gold color, precisely the color I want my hair in my next incarnation. It was as soft and almost as weightless as whipped cream, and as warm as Cancún. And it was only fifteen dollars, half the price of the neighboring down and woolen garments. The label said Paris.

Wondering, I bought it. Presently I stopped wondering: it was cheap because there's no place to wear it.

Well, not quite no place. I can wear it at home when the furnace goes off, or in the woods when I go out to clear brush. Here where

I live, in deer- and squirrel-hunting country, I can wear it as far as the hardware store but no closer than that to the city. In the city, nice people don't wear fur, and they've been known to attack not-nice people.

When it gets really viciously cold — fur-coat cold — nice people wear goose-down coats and vests, trundling along the streets like walking fire hydrants. (I have no idea how the down is removed from the goose, but I bet it hurts.) Or they wear the new synthetic fabrics with capitalized names, which may be scientific insulation but can hardly be called a pleasure; they have all the sensuous satisfaction of a canvas mailbag. Fur coats — inarguably the best, softest, warmest, most comfortable and water-resistant of winter clothing — languish in the backs of closets or travel, under cover of darkness, to thrift shops.

Fur is our most ancient garment, our first covering, the portable warmth that let us leave the fire at the mouth of the cave and go out to find our dinner; to build ships and explore the world. Fire set us free from the equatorial regions, but fur set us free from fire. It saved our lives for all those uncountable centuries before spinning wheels and looms, and we have deep, long reasons to love it. Huddling our shoulders into it, wrapping it across the chest, smiling involuntarily at its touch, we're in direct contact with the Oldest Ones.

It seems sad to break so radically with our past, but I bow to the angry forces of moral superiority. I bow, but I don't understand. I heartily believe that it's wrong to trap wild animals for fur; wild animals have a right to their anxious, hardscrabble lives. I just don't understand the distinction between raising sheep — amiable, if dimwitted, creatures — for their lamb chops and raising mink — evil-tempered, foul-smelling animals related to polecats — for their fur.

Of course there are those who don't eat lamb chops, for moral reasons. There are also those who rise before daybreak and leap into a cold shower in February; those who disapprove of idleness, gin rummy, slang, dancing, unauthorized sex, naps, socialism, and Jacuzzis for moral reasons. They enjoy it; moral indignation is a pleasure, often the only pleasure, in many lives. It's also one of the few pleasures people feel obliged to force on other people.

I spread the rabbit jacket across my lap, in the privacy of my own home, and brush my hand across its golden wealth of softness. I feel regretful on its behalf; being from Paris, it probably longs for an evening at the theater or a stroll along the boulevards. Alas, I am a coward. Perhaps next winter I'll turn it inside out and wear it to bed — a prospect so outrageously delicious that even I could almost disapprove.

Color

ALL winter I court cardinals, shamelessly. (The birds, that is, not the clerics; a passing College of Cardinals in full-dress hats would be a fine sight too, but harder to lure to Virginia.) I court the birds with the priciest sunflower seeds, dragged home from the store and spread freshly two or three times a day. It's expensive and time-consuming, but well worth it, because cardinals, male cardinals, are red.

Considered purely as creatures, they aren't much. They're quarrelsome, timid, and stupid, compared to the brave, resourceful chickadee, for instance, and always the first to scatter at some imaginary alarm and the last to come back, leaving the chickadees in charge. But chickadees are only black and gray, and in the black-and-gray winter landscape I crave red as desert travelers crave water. I could get in the car and go look for a red stop sign, or even a yellow school bus, but being lazy, I stay home and put out sun-flower seeds so the red will come to me. A cardinal in a slant of winter sunlight goes straight to the bloodstream like brandy, and the heart leaps up like a startled stag.

I don't know what it is about color. Anthropologist Lionel Tiger, analyzing our joys in *The Pursuit of Pleasure*, says that the absence of color, the application of drab muncipal hues, is used by repres-sive governments to keep the masses in line. In *The Anatomy of Melancholy*, the seventeenth-century sage Robert Burton, speaking on cures for depression, says, "Of colors, it is good to behold green, red, yellow, and white. . . ." In *33 Happy Moments,* the wise Chin Shengt'ans muses, "To cut with a sharp knife a bright green water-melon on a big scarlet plate of a summer afternoon. Ah, is not this happiness?" Obviously, a gray watermelon on a tan plate wouldn't pack the same punch.

All our pleasure responses are supposed to have been adaptive at one point, helping us up the evolutionary ladder, but I don't see how red fits into this theory.

Blue I can understand. John Ruskin, lecturing on painting, said, "Blue colour is everlastingly appointed by the Deity to be a source of delight." Whether or not the Deity was involved, blue skies have always meant good weather. Red, though, couldn't have helped us stalk the woolly mammoth or learn to plant grain. Maybe color is a very pure, purposeless joy, existing for the sake of joy alone.

We don't seem to be alone in our taste for color. Why would a cardinal bother to be red if red didn't matter to its world? Why would a rose? Except for a handful of morbidly cultivated tulips, there are no black flowers; apparently even the utilitarian bee likes a touch of color in its day. Farmers, not known as a class for their esthetic sense, paint their barns red so they can look at them and take cheer through the long gray winters.

Color excites and pleases us so much that it's officially repressed or rationed in anti-pleasure circles. Quakers wore gray to keep their minds off frivolous matters. Lawyers have a taste for black suits, to indicate strict mental efficiency, and priests — except for the above-mentioned Cardinals, presumably so far above the lower clerical ranks that they can handle a splash of red without losing their cool — wear black. Oliver Cromwell and his gloomy followers wore black. Women in strict Islamic countries wear black by law. In many times and societies, nice women never, never wore red, because of its suggestive and exciting properties; Hester Prynne's letter "A" was scarlet.

In the visual deprivation of winter, when we need a bit of naughty stimulation, we lure red birds to the back porch. They sit on the railing, not singing sweetly, not flying gracefully, not doing anything remarkable except being as red as a peal of trumpets.

Sometimes I think it would be easier to paint the living-room walls red, along about the first of December. Then I could cover the red with hopeful canary yellow in April, and go back to cool, unstimulating ivory in the sensual month of June, when flowers bloom and the system needs no extra jolt.

The cardinals would be disappointed, though. They've learned to expect being courted. Come to think of it, maybe red has been evolutionarily adaptive for cardinals, at least since the invention of bird feeders

Christmas

BECAUSE Christmas is generally accepted as pleasure's pinnacle, the happiest day of the year, it causes widespread and sometimes fatal depression. Many adults look forward to it and its aftermath as to dental surgery, but somehow, even if no bright-eyed tots expect it of them, they continue to go through the motions, some for religious reasons, some simply because it's the custom, and some, with ethnic roots in northern countries, because their genes insist on marking the winter solstice. Even though we now know with fair certainty that the sun won't desert us forever, leaving utter darkness to swallow the land, the returning minutes of daylight flood us with secret relief. As Solomon put it, "The light is sweet, and it is delightful for the eyes to see the sun."

So, doggedly, we keep on celebrating.

The most hellish aspect of the modern Christmas is its crushing burden of travel. Due to the decline in American family values, when we marry we no longer add a bedroom to our parents' farmhouse and stay there forever. We no longer go over the river and through the woods to grandmother's house. Indeed, we may be expected, like Santa Claus himself, to visit every state in the union at precisely the same moment.

Without half trying, we can easily have two sets of parents and four sets of grandparents, possibly a living great-grandparent. Then we marry someone with similar baggage, which gives us fourteen households from Ft. Lauderdale to Seattle, San Diego to Boston, where feelings will be hurt if we don't come down the chimney on time and bring the kids. It can't be done. Relatives take umbrage. They refuse to play second fiddle, or eleventh fiddle, and take us for Thanksgiving — or Flag Day or Guy Fawkes Day — instead. Their pride is hurt, and they sulk, which makes us feel so guilty that we turn around and smack the kids on this the happiest day of the year. Presently — perhaps shortly after Christmas — we get a divorce, and now the kids' father and new stepmother expect them for Christmas in Chicago, as well as our own new husband's mother and stepfather in Tucson and our father and stepmother in Cleveland and all the rest of the gang.

It's quite possible to spend all but a couple of the twenty-four hours of Christmas in airports. (The remaining two hours are spent in a rented car in a sleet storm, with the dog throwing up all over the gaily wrapped presents and our spouse taking nips from a flask.) Even so we will have fallen short of our visiting duty and opened familial rifts that will need repairing, and we're probably coming down with flu.

This is what comes of piling so many expectations onto such a slender reed, all jammed together like angels on the head of a pin. So many weeks of anticipation, so much money spent, so many clothes purchased, trees trimmed, cards mailed, wreaths hung, turkeys basted, songs sung, and all to be snatched away in a wink, or gulped down by a traffic jam or a flight schedule. It's gone, all this legendary happiness, for another twelve months; we grabbed for it but it slipped from our hand somehow, and that was all there was. Was this a metaphor for our whole lives, this certainty of joy, this dream of perfect happiness and love, annually torn from our lips before we can taste it? Perhaps we should put our heads in the gas oven after all, or at any rate have a couple more drinks.

How could our ancestors have enjoyed it so thoroughly? You can tell they did; listen to the rollick of their Christmas songs, the merry gentlemen, the wassail bowl, the decked halls. Consider the games, the dancing, the great long tables sagging under geese and pigs and peacocks, the general merriment in hall and hovel alike. They were having fun.

The answer, and the cure for our own ills, is perfectly simple: it lasted longer then. It lasted so long that you could come down with a bad cold and be well again before you'd missed it all. You could visit everyone. By *train*, if necessary — if they'd had such a thing as trains.

"On the twelfth day of Christmas my true love gave to me twelve ladies dancing, eleven lords a-leaping, ten drummers drumming, nine pipers piping, eight maids a-milking, seven swans a-swimming, six geese a-laying, five golden rings, four colly birds, three French hens, two turtledoves, and a partridge in a pear tree." For loot and longevity, that beat even Hannukah.

Both as a pre-Christian rejoicing at the return of daylight and later, as a Christian, rather arbitrarily chosen, celebration superimposed on the older festival, it roistered on and on. The Roman saturnalia lasted only a week, but other countries managed to stretch out the carousing through the first week of January. In an agrarian society the lull between harvest and planting was nature's holiday. Cows still had to be milked and chickens fed, but that was child's play compared to the long hours of back-breaking field work. At December's end, if half the village was drunk by noon it was no great loss.

Such a fine time was had by all that the wise Pope Gregory I decreed in 601 that everyone should go right on roistering, only changing the object of their celebrations, and "still keeping outward pleasures, they may more readily receive spiritual joys." (It's possible there were certain aspects of the festival that nobody'd had the heart to tell him about.)

From the eleventh to the seventeenth century, Christmas in the British Isles and through much of Europe lasted till Twelfth Night and everyone gained a shocking amount of weight, eating and drinking pretty much nonstop; that ceremonial boar's head was only an hors d'oeuvre. There were towering bonfires to encourage the sun, and smooching and goosing under the mistletoe to encourage fertility, and such a proliferation of games, masques, hospitalities, plays, jesters, minstrels, dances, punch bowls, giggling, and songs that it's no wonder the Puritans, who loathed fun, outlawed the whole disorderly feast in 1644.

Charles II's Restoration brought it back but it was never quite the same, and then the Industrial Revolution condensed it into the paltry twenty-four hours we scramble through today. A factory is not a farm, and factory owners simply couldn't bear the thought of a long winter festival, with profits dwindling and workers wandering about wassailing for days on end. Accordingly, they invoked Cromwell's Puritans, and much was, and still is, preached about the "true spirit of Christmas," by which employers mean going to church, eating dinner, and punching the time clock early and sober on the *very next day*. Scrooge lives.

Naturally we're depressed. You could almost say we've been robbed of our birthright, and you could certainly say we've been lied to. This is *not the true spirit of Christmas*, which traditionally since its very beginning involved more merrymaking, thanks to Gregory the Great, than sermons.

I suggest a rebellion. Or perhaps just a gradual, evolutionary return to tradition, under which we erode a couple of work-weeks. Take the extra day, then two; come in late, leave early, hang mistletoe over our desks, encourage sexual harassment, singing, perhaps a small bonfire in the employees' cafeteria, a bowl of wassail in the boardroom.

Future generations will bless us, and the rest of the winter, from Twelfth Night on, will be all the sweeter, pass all the more swiftly, after a good old-fashioned Christmas fortnight.

Pampering

WE don't get enough pampering. If we were once the only child of an adoring mother, we developed a taste for it; if not, we developed a thirst for it. Grown up, we went looking for it and found it in short supply. It's hard even to find someone to wash our back anymore, let alone make chicken soup. Everyone's busy.

Husbands used to get pampered by their wives; husband-pampering was a girl's most important lesson and included everything from ironing the perfect shirt to rubbing the back of the husbandly neck to ease the day's tensions. It must have been heaven to be a husband a generation or two ago. The home, the entire functioning of daily life, was arranged to satisfy his whims and crotchets; small children hushed at his footfall; eggs were cooked to his specifications; and should he take to his bed with flu he was tended and babied like an orchid, his brow stroked, his pillows plumped. It's hard to believe now that half the population was once appointed to pamper the other half, but at least back then half the population *did* get some care and attention. Now nobody does, and we all long for it.

We long for it guiltily. It's out of key with the current Spartan state of the nation. We shouldn't want to be cosseted, we should want stress, challenge, activity, self-denial, independence. Aerobics have replaced the rest cure.

Sometimes advertisers of luxury goods urge us to pamper ourselves, but pampering, like praise, is more effective when someone else does it for us. Does it exclusively for love of us — unlike the advertisers who, we suspect, don't even know our names and may be interested only in our money.

What we miss is the sense that somebody out there cares about our physical comfort and pleasure. We've pretty much pared this down to sex, which takes less time than chicken soup but isn't quite the same, since ideally both parties enjoy it equally. The essence of pampering is that the other person is doing it solely in order to make *us* feel good, which may be selfish, but what else is new?

Happily, when we try to stamp out our natural longings, they pop back up again disguised and rationalized. Massage technique is flourishing. We tell each other that massage is good for us, medicine instead of indulgence, and roll up our sleeves and rub each other. Where once was just the friendly back-rub, we now have oils and ointments, shiatsu and several other Oriental types, reflexology, Swedish, deep-muscle, head-and-face and specific-therapy massage. Sometimes, at the higher levels, it hurts, but the personal attention being paid to our bodies makes up for the pain.

If we can't find anyone willing to rub us, we can go to a spa and get rubbed. Spas fall into two categories: the American, or punitive, and the European, or pampering. The American style focuses on prolonged exercise and virtually nothing to eat, with massage added strictly for recovery from yesterday's exercise so we can face today's. But it still means that someone notices and cares, cares enough to scold and beat and starve our flesh for its own good. The European type coddles the customer more gently and bundles it in seaweed. Sweetly, clothed in a soft robe instead of a warm-up suit, the client is led through a symphony of baths and rinses and oilings and body-wraps and sweet smells and expert rubbings, then fed a delicious lunch custom-tailored by coddlers in the kitchen.

Elements of the European have invaded some of the American spas, and on both sides there may be magical muds or waters to add to the mystique. I'm sure all of these services are just as medicinal as claimed, if only for the heart-stirring, soul-fattening attention they lay on. Not since we were toilet-trained has anyone focused so intently on our flesh.

If we can't afford a spa, and have medical insurance, we can get sick enough to be hospitalized. The food's terrible and the care may be brusque, but at least someone's paying attention to our physical self, and taking its temperature and writing it down on a chart.

We talk and read about and take courses on caring for each other's emotions and communicating our own, but back when we began this journey through our days we didn't give a fig for emotions. We'd never heard of them. All we knew was our flesh, and having someone feed its inside and rub its outside down with baby oil and wrap it in a blanket. It felt good. It still does. The flesh is us.

Praise

MRS. CASEY taught tenth-grade English, and she was a teacher in the grand tradition, small, neat, severe, and opinionated. Her sarcasm was famous. She never complimented me, or anyone, in class, though after she'd elicited a string of foolish answers she would sometimes sigh, close her eyes briefly, and call on me, whether or not my hand was raised, with a note of finality in her voice. This was heady stuff, but the peak — the high point of my school days, in fact — came when she signaled me to stop at her desk after class. She was scribbling on a slip of paper.

"You needn't," she said crisply, "come to class next week. Here's a library pass. I'm having them do a reading of *Julius Caesar*, which would be just as painful for you as for me. However, I get paid for it and you don't." She held out the slip.

Come to think of it, perhaps this was the pinnacle of my entire career, or even my entire life. Dizzy, I inhaled it deeply and handed back the pass. "I'll come to class," I said, "if I can read Mark Antony."

She tore it up. "Thank you," she said, unsmiling. "That will make it easier for me." She busied herself with papers and I was dismissed, drunk and staggering through the halls. The high lasted for weeks.

Recently, praise has been making headlines as a cure for most of what's wrong with the country, promoting what's called "self-esteem," a lack of which seems to be the root of all evil. An expensive study concluded that students who thought highly of themselves were getting better grades than those who didn't, and it never crossed anyone's mind that they might have admired themselves because they were good instead of the other way around.

The state of California, as usual, is spearheading the movement with a rash of praise programs and local self-esteem task forces. Schools, parents, employers, and even prisons everywhere are ladling out admiration to all comers. All of us are encouraged to feel marvelous about ourselves, praising ourselves daily when no one else can be persuaded to do it.

The ancient custom of awarding a medal to the Best Student left too many students unmedaled and at risk for lowered self-esteem, so now awards must be invented for all. The Best Student, once the star, is now but one of a multitude, and why struggle for scholarship when you're sure of an award for something, if only the Cleanest Fingernails or Best Ten-Year-Old Hopscotch Player? Triumph spread too thin is flavorless.

Feeling that we're wonderful usually involves feeling rather more wonderful than the next man; this is basic to human nature and the whole point of spelling bees, baseball, the Nobel Prize, the Miss America contest, television ratings, and the Olympic Games. If all of us are wonderful, then each is merely average, which is much less fun. The most treasured word from Mrs. Casey was "them": "I'm having *them* do a reading." I was me, the rest were merely them.

We're told that if we remind our mirrors every morning that we are very, very special people our self-esteem will leap to attention and our incomes skyrocket accordingly, but most of us aren't that gullible: our mirrors just laugh. Praise isn't a pleasure we can arrange for ourselves, like a hot bath or a comfortable chair. It really needs to be delivered by someone else, and much of its impact depends on the deliverer. I was praised by others after Mrs. Casey, but never to quite the same effect — from her, the compliment was wrung grudgingly, like squeezing wine from a stone, and besides, she knew whereof she spoke. A nod of satisfaction from an expert carries more weight than eulogies from the ignorant.

Hardest of all to arrange, we should feel the words are justified. A compliment on my singing voice, for instance, would be sarcasm, not praise — though once someone did say, "You don't sing *that* badly," and it gave me quite a glow.

Another sticking point is the value we place on the attribute. Go up to an anxious young artist at his first one-man show and tell him he's wearing a swell tie and see how his self-esteem takes it.

Also, if possible, the quality should be our own, not just an attachment: "What a pretty dress" doesn't cheer like "Don't you look delicious tonight"; anyone can buy a pretty dress, but it takes talent to look delicious.

All things considered, praise is an elusive pleasure. Best not to count on it. Still, when it does come, we can wallow in it thoroughly, roll around in it, drag it into conversations, crow into our pillows, install it in the heart, engrave it on the brain, and whisper it over and over to ourselves before we go to sleep. It feels wonderful.

Self-esteem, once called "conceit," is something else again. I'm not sure it's the panacea California thinks it is.

Relief

MANY of life's most treasured moments are perhaps better described as relief than pleasure; they were paid for in advance, but they're no less pleasurable for it. This is the class of happiness experienced by, for instance, plane passengers who, immediately after the landing, are giving the pilot a standing ovation, cheering, stomping, whistling, and embracing one another in the aisles.

Our days are filled with these moments, large and small and all worth celebrating, though some would consider them negative, as in "negative lab test." The dentist found no new cavities; the jury found us innocent; our in-laws changed their plans for a visit, or did visit and have now departed. The baby has finally stopped crying and, still sweaty and shuddering, gone to sleep. The men with the jackhammers have laid them down and opened their lunch pails.

It wasn't the transmission after all. The burglar downstairs turned out to be mice. Our teenaged daughter is not pregnant by a druggy-looking biker with no visible means of support. The power came back on before the pipes froze. The check didn't bounce. Our secret is safe and the incriminating film has been destroyed. Nobody notices that dinner has been dropped on the kitchen floor; the brush fire is quickly put out with a garden hose; our lovers are late arriving only because their cars broke down. The lost cat came back, hungry and glad to see us. Our fever has gone down and we might eat a little something. We drove home on ice, white-knuckled and fishtailing, dodging wrecks, chin on the steering wheel, and got there; waded through the drifts, let ourself in, poured a stiff drink and took off the wet shoes and the socks caked with ice chunks. Put on fleece-lined slippers. Built a fire.

The income-tax forms are baled up and ready to ship to the IRS. The footsteps behind us in the dark have turned down another street. The plane landed intact.

The bluebird of happiness may be rare and fleeting, but the white dove of relief brushes our brows pretty often and deserves a welcome. Even if its price was in-laws visiting or a fever of 103.

Disasters

DISASTERS are fun. They're fun to watch on television: see the reporter on the boardwalk, trenchcoat whipping in the wind, reporting on the beachfront's evacuation as the hurricane draws nigh. See the flattened prairie town, aerial view of mangled trailer parks, roofless supermarket, uprooted trees in the wake of the tornado. See the Gulf War, by the rockets' red glare, the bombs bursting in air. See the volunteers digging in the rubble for earthquake victims; see the fallen forest on Mount Saint Helens. All fun.

Misanthropes claim we enjoy these things because we were spared, mean-spiritedly rejoicing that someone else's home, not ours, stood in the path of the forest fire. I don't think that's true. I think that we, who sometimes pay hard cash to be frightened out of our senses on the roller-coaster, simply need excitement. Our lives used to be very exciting indeed, dodging saber-toothed tigers and wondering whether we'd freeze before we starved and whether the spirits of our ancestors might choke us to death in the night. Our adrenaline *likes* to be kick-started; it evolved that way.

We can spend money to go hang-gliding or rock-climbing or, for free, we can cross the street against the light. If we're president, we can start a war. If we're an arsonist, we can start a fire. But most of us risk our lives only by eating animal fats and breathing second-hand cigarette smoke, and somehow this doesn't give us that bracing frisson of terror that was once a part of our daily world. Then, occasionally, for a treat, we're offered a disaster to send us soaring out of our boring safety.

Those who were brought up with proper consciences wring their hands and murmur, "Oh, those poor people, think of the suffering," but in their hearts they too enjoy. We even enjoy it in our own back yard, as long as we don't actually get maimed or lose too much irreplaceable property. If we have a long warning, as with the average blizzard, hurricane, or war, we can bustle around making preparations as if for a party, laying in stores of bread and beer and baby formula, tying yellow ribbons on the mailbox, boarding up the windows, lashing down the trash cans, blood racing with anticipation. If whatever it was doesn't live up to expectations, the foot of snow less than an inch, the hurricane a windy drizzle, the war a walkaway, we're disappointed. We feel as if we'd paid to see the Fat Lady in the sideshow and she was barely fatter than Aunt Alma; we'd wanted her to be *huge*; immensely, breathtakingly fat. We like extremes; they're exciting.

We like a solid, full-blown disaster. It's cathartic. The earth heaves and brings forth a monster. Houses fall down. Waves crash through the city streets. Flames lick the sky. And it's real, all real, not a movie or the Old Testament: the world, that yesterday seemed so flat and predictable, lights up as a dangerous and dramatic place to live, and some of the glow falls into our own lives. We feel freshened, stretched and taller, in a landscape where such things can happen.

Of course, some disasters are more fun than others, and the best are over when they're over. Chernobyl was not a pleasurable happening. It was sinister. Nothing to look at, no flames, no floodwaters, just an invisible cloud carrying nasty, creeping doom wherever the wind sent it wandering, poisoning Santa's reindeer in innocent, snowy Lapland, dragging on forever in the victims' lives. No proper sense of theater at all.

The excitement we thirst for goes bang or whoosh and then passes on, leaving us, if we were close enough, gathered in excited, chattering groups around the wreckage, crunching broken glass underfoot, waiting for the television crews to ask us questions, hoping to be on the evening news. The evening news that the rest of us watch so avidly, drinking in those good old cataclysms that we crave.

There's absolutely nothing wrong with this; it's one of our most natural pleasures. Excitement was mother's milk to the human race, and made us quick and canny. Nowadays we have to take it where we can find it.

The downside of this metabolic urge is that, when life has flattened and grayed beyond endurance, we stir up our own bloodstreams. Lacking natural bangs and crashes, we create them with everything from hallucinogens to beer-inspired fistfights. These seem to be a natural reaction to peacetime, the absence of predators, and the orderly life. Not much can be done about them; they're an old as — and possibly the result of — civilization. If the much-advertised war on drugs is ever won, heaven knows what we'll think up next.

Crowds

BEING a physical part of a like-minded, many-headed multitude is one of our trashiest thrills. Intellectuals pride themselves on immunity; all of us are mildly embarrassed by it, but what can you do? We're tribal creatures.

When we say we hate crowds, we mean crowds with whom we have nothing in common beyond the common urge to get to Forty-second Street on the subway or the tenth floor in the elevator, or to finish our Christmas shopping. Thrilling crowds, crowds that stir our blood in low and primitive ways, are those that share our current purpose or feeling, heightening and reinforcing it. We're all together in this — we're here to watch the home team win, or to establish or abolish abortion rights, elect our candidate, protest a war, or break into the jailhouse and lynch the prisoner, and what may have started as only a tepid interest is whipped into white-hot excitement by the presence of our fellow-man in bulk. Watching it on television, even live television, is not the same as being there. The lone fan on his living-room couch screaming "Beat Yale! Beat Yale!" simply isn't screwed up to the same fever pitch as the fan in a host of fans. Imagine a one-man Ku Klux Klan. A one-man Woodstock.

Excitement flicks through us like an electric current and welds us, for better or worse, into an almost sexual unit, which is why it's dangerous to attend soccer games. After this mass orgasm we feel let down, spent, purged, disheveled, hungover, but while it lasted it was an authentic, if shameful, pleasure. We'd been tired of being alone, even alone among our emotionally various fellow-workers or families with their separate agendas; we'd yearned to shout with a common voice. It doesn't much matter whether we were chanting "Stop the war" or "Kill kill kill kill" or "God save the Queen." Any shout will do. You might argue that it helps our pride to have been shouting in a virtuous crusade, but with a large enough crowd, any old crusade feels virtuous.

When President Kennedy was shot we should, if we were a rational animal, have wanted to be alone, or perhaps with a few intimate friends. Sit quietly in a dark room, musing on this watershed tragedy. We didn't, though. We poured out into the streets to form a crowd. Apartment and office buildings emptied, parks and sidewalks filled. Stumbling, bemused, we milled aimlessly among our aimlessly milling fellows. So many of us, all reeling from the same shock. And underlying our grief was this inadmissible pleasure of being at one with a great multitude.

It's a dangerous drug. It makes us malleable. Face to face with, say, Adolf Hitler at a table for two, we would have jeered at his passions, protested, flounced out in a snit. In a crowd of thousands, all cheering and brandishing fists, we might have stood in the path of the electric current, felt the blood of common cause rise joyfully in our throats, and cheered too. It's the same pleasure, after all, that brings us to our feet for the ovation after a brilliant symphony; how foolish, how lonely we'd feel, just sitting there placidly smiling; how happy it makes us to join in.

Deep inside each of us lurks a chained lemming, struggling to break free, and we need to keep an eye on it.

Birds

BIRDS fly better than we do. More gracefully, less expensively. Some people keep birds in cages, perhaps in a deliberate move to cut off their superiority in this matter: You think you're so talented, parakeet? Take that! *Now* let's see you go swooping through the air. A bird in a cage, hopping six inches from perch to swing and back again, has been shorn of its birdliness; it might as well be a gerbil. Man triumphant.

A bird in the hand is worth two in the bush, and also a curious and exciting sensation, all powdery, shifting feathers, frantic heartbeat, glaring eyes, panting beak. This is not a warm, consoling puppy we're holding; it isn't even a mammal. Birds are different.

They live in an extra dimension. So do fish, of course, but it's hard to imagine life as a fish. Nobody knows what a fish thinks or how it feels, while all of us know how a bird feels, from our daydreams and night dreams: it feels wonderful. It's not afraid of falling. It plays in thin air. Gulls, hawks, and condors float on it, sensitive to its kind support under the curve of their wings. Birds have no use for elevators, swings, seesaws, 747s, parachutes, extension ladders, staircases, cherry-pickers, or bungee-jumping. They don't need safety-nets against the gravity that lies in wait for the rest of us, ready to snatch us down and nail us to the earth. When the north turns dark and disagreeable, some birds simply go south for the winter, like millionaires, while we stay behind and trudge heavily, step by step, along the icy sidewalks. It's annoying.

As children, we all climb up on chairs or tree stumps and jump off, flapping our arms, and land hard. Particularly in Britain, I understand, small boys succumb to an irresistible urge to steal birds' eggs from nests, as if to possess the seed or possibility of becoming a bird.

As we get older, if we're modest and humble we accept our inferiority and rejoice in watching birds do what we can't do. Can't possibly do, ever. It's not likely we will ever pitch a no-hitter against the Orioles or pole-vault ten feet, but we can try, we can practice. We will never be able to fly. If we're more normal, we're bitter about it, ignore birds whenever possible, and speak slightingly of their intellectual life. (Which would you really rather do, fly or read Cicero's *De Oratore*?)

We retaliate by inventing angels and fairies, humanoids who can fly like birds. Angels are said to be the apotheosis of human perfection, so we've given them the one thing we so clearly lack and so badly want. (It would be nice to have fur too, short and dense and soft as a rabbit's, all over our bare, wrinkly skin; we could sit around stroking ourselves, and make love to other softly furred humans. Still, we can keep warm without fur. We can't fly without wings. We're always just Icarus, crashing back to earth in man-made feathers, punished for hubris, for jealousy.)

No wonder so many of us, shut out, feel sourly indifferent to the bird world. Bird-watchers, or "birders," go to great lengths to find and look at them, but mostly in a pragmatic spirit. The basic bird-watcher isn't watching so much as counting and listing. Imposing a kind of human order on the anarchic world of wings. Sorting and naming.

As with the rest of us creatures, there are glamour birds and trash birds, at least in our eyes. Meadowlarks and buzzards. Whooping cranes and starlings. Condors and pigeons.

In the cities we stride through the park and dislodge whole flapping blankets of pigeons, and complain about the mess they make. Sky-rats, we call them. Vermin. This is sad, because, aside from cockroaches, pigeons are the basic urban wildlife, and we need a bit of wildlife around. If, instead of just burbling lecherously in springtime, pigeons sang as sweetly as wood thrushes, I suppose we'd feel better about them, and cities in May would ring like celestial cathedrals. People would stand still on the sidewalks, smiling to hear the pigeons sing.

Some birds, in addition to flying, sing better than we do. Even the most unmusical among us notices, at some subliminal level, the spring birdsongs, but we can't resent them because they're so clearly a joyful noise unto the Lord. For birds that wintered over, life has eased up; for the migrants, it's nice to be back home. They sing, apparently, two basic songs: "I am the king! the king! the king!" and "Wherever you are, I love you." (It's possible, though unscientific, that they also sing because they enjoy making such fine music; I would.) Whether we're consciously listening or not, these messages make us happy, even in a spring drizzle with our feet wet. Happiness is highly contagious.

Most birds live short lives. They're apt to freeze, starve, and have their homes destroyed by the fierce encroachments of man, but since they don't know this in advance, it doesn't worry them. They go right on singing and flying. They've even been seen playing.

I once spent most of an afternoon watching a party of barn swallows playing with a swimming pool. They gathered around the deep end and took turns flying the length of the pool, swooping low over it. Any scientist would assure me they were hunting insects, but it was a breezy, bugless day, and no bird was seen catching a bug, and they flew in a straight line down the middle of the pool, which is no way to hunt. The game was obviously a form of chicken and the point was to fly as close as possible to the water without hitting it. From time to time one of them did splash down, and the others, I assumed, laughed uproariously in barn-swallow.

One man I knew, a stern, unsentimental fellow, swears he watched a group of small birds, exact type unknown, sliding on their bellies down an icy patch of lawn, over and over for an hour.

It's entirely possible that being a bird is just as much fun as we've always thought it would be.

If we can suppress our honest, justified envy, the idea, the existence, of birds is a pleasure, a joy to eye and ear and an inspiration to daydreams. If nature hadn't provided them, I suppose some human genius would have invented them, and the concept would have dazzled us all.

Dogs

FOR longer than either of us can remember, dogs have been a source of pleasure for humans. The all-purpose pet, they were useful in hunting, served as an extra blanket on cold nights, tidied up the garbage, and when game was scarce — or even when it wasn't — we could eat them. (It was Scott's reluctance and Amundsen's willingness to boil up their four-footed friends that got Amundsen home safe from the South Pole and left Scott freezing in his tent. Critics said Amundsen wasn't a real gentleman like Scott, since no real gentleman would dream of such a thing. Amundsen just smiled.)

Most of us now, except in wartime, can afford to wax sentimental about our dogs and feed them rather than eat them. The dogs in return feel equally sentimental about us, and greet us as if we were Odysseus when we come back home from the front porch. This ego-enhancement outweighs even the joys of hunting, warmth, and stew.

Almost any dog thinks almost any human is the Great Spirit, the Primal Creator, and the Universal Force Behind the Sun and Tides. What human can resist? When the day at the office has been evil, our labors belittled and our inferiors preferred above us, Spot rushes to greet us with explosive relief and paroxysms of joy, often shedding a few drops of urine on the floor as if they were tears of pure gladness. If we are hours late getting home and without a decent excuse to offer, Spot's stomach is empty and her bladder full, but no word of reproach is uttered and her gladness is undimmed; few others in life will pile adoration on our heads in return for abuse. Spot may even sit when we tell her to. Lamentably few spouses rush to the door wriggling with delight these days, and almost none of them sit on command any more; Spot is a pearl beyond price. A poultice over the wounds of the day.

Much is made of the pleasures of parenthood, and children do have their points, but how many of our young deeply, sincerely, believe that we alone cause the sun to shine and the fields to yield forth their crops? How many even glance up from the television to note our triumphal return, and of those who do, how many say, "What did you bring me?"

We may be miserly, spiteful, flatulent, balding, and fat, with disgusting table manners and a snore that rattles the bed, but our dog doesn't merely overlook these traits, she considers them evidence of Godhead. Is it any wonder so many people are replacing their families altogether with dogs, superior in so many ways, including admiration, loyalty, initial cost, upkeep, and sleeping habits?

As a confidant, the dog has no peer, listening attentively but never leaking our lurid past to the tabloids. As a companion, the dog gladly accepts our agenda and never wants to go shopping instead. As security, the dog — well, sometimes — defends the home against burglars and mailmen and the jogger against panhandlers. As helpmeet, the dog never chatters distractingly or tells us we're doing it wrong. And, as mentioned before, it serves as an ambulant cache of high-protein emergency rations in case of siege or famine. Few simple pleasures are as broadly rewarding.

Cats

FOR some people, the pet dog is just a bit too, well, *predictable*. Once you have come to know your dog and the one or two ways in which she differs from thousands or perhaps millions of other dogs, she's unlikely to astonish you; she's the same all the way through, like a banana. The cat is layered, like an artichoke.

Pleasingly, the outermost layer is fur. (Most dogs, too, are furred, but the product varies in quality, texture, density, and, lamentably, smell.) Naked ourselves, we long for fur. Fur is superior to human skin in every cosmetic and practical respect; it insulates the flesh, resists sunburn, and doesn't show wrinkles, bruises, acne, sweat, or cellulite. It looks much the same in old age as in youth. It feels good, too. We like to touch it, but in recent years a cloud (see WEARING FUR) has fallen over the ancient custom of appropriating animal furs and swaggering around pretending they're ours. If we're going to run our hands over fur, it's now correct only if the creature's still in it. (Actually, it feels better that way, the creature adding a warmth and solidity under the softness.)

For fur on the hoof, you can't beat a cat. It's exactly the right size to have around the house, it's naturally clean in its habits, and if it likes you it sometimes gives off a nice humming sound. In the winter, it's better to sleep with than a hot-water bottle, maintaining an even temperature all night and never slipping off the foot of the bed and dragging the blankets off with it. On the lap, a cat far outshines a child; it's lighter in weight and softer to touch, and doesn't whine, squirm, or object to having a book propped on its back.

If your relationship with the cat goes beyond the purely physical, you'll uncover a few more layers under the fur, though being but human you'll never penetrate clear to the intricate prickly geometry of the choke and the hidden heart under it. However, your cat, unlike your dog, will sometimes astonish you. Sometimes its mental processes will impress you. Sometimes it will simply baffle you, as in the matter of Jeoffrey and the shower.

Jeoffrey is a young Siamese, overweight, placid, and rather timid, with a consuming passion for people showering or, more precisely, people who have showered. The first sound the showerer hears after turning off the water is Jeoffrey shrieking and clawing frantically at the door. The door must be opened, *has* to be opened, on even the shyest guest, or Jeoffrey will tear it down. Once inside the steamy, damp bathroom, he purrs thunderously, trembling with pleasure, and rubs against the wet legs over and over, pausing to turn an occasional somersault of pure joy. When he's dried the legs to cat-height, he hops into the wet bathtub and dries that, still ecstatic, still purring.

Finally the bemused showerer puts on a bathrobe and emerges, accompanied by steam and Jeoffrey, who strolls across the hall with the drunken dignity of a deacon leaving a brothel.

I don't understand, but the occasional mystery, the otherness of cats, is part of their charm. Humans and dogs are all very well, but their familiarity breeds contempt. No one feels too familiar with a cat. Cats provide a needed outlet for the human imagination.

Or, if we feel we have enough to wonder about already, we can limit our examination to the fur; it's almost excuse enough for cats.

Wild Animals

SECRETLY, even the most scornful of skeptics would like to believe in extraterrestrial beings. We're sick and tired of living all alone here with only ourselves to talk to, and we long for a spot of adult companionship. Besides, extraterrestrials obviously know useful things that we don't know, like how to travel comfortably among planets and how to sustain an advanced technological civilization that hasn't torn itself to bits in bad-tempered ethnic, religious, or patriotic spats.

We're not likely to listen to our own advice, but theirs would be worth hearing. And we already know all about each other, but they'd bring strange and different things to teach us, new stories to tell, exotic food and drink and artwork; we yearn for their news as islanders yearn for mail.

In the meantime, though, while we wait and scan the skies, we can think about wild animals, which were here before we were and are still out there somewhere.

Wild animals are different from dogs and cows; they're adults like us. Pets and farm animals are children under our care, irresponsibly leaning on us for food and shelter and instructions, while even the smallest tree-toad in the woods earns his independent living and copes with his own existence in spite of rather than because of us.

Probably we'll never be able to talk to wild animals, and I can't imagine why they'd listen if we could. I don't know what we'd learn from them; they'd have no useful technological tips for us, and such physical tricks as hibernating, flying, and digesting grass are probably unteachable. And it's improbable that they'll teach us to mend our social manners; would we learn to be as lovingly cooperative as a meerkat colony or as morosely lone and territorial as leopards? I suppose we have our own species-specific manners and we're stuck with them.

Still, animals, independent animals, are good company to think about sometimes, when we get bored with ourselves. They're a toy for the mind. They're restful: we know they have their own problems, but problems don't much worry them ahead of time, and they don't have to waste their days in niggling occupations like checking the batteries in the smoke-detectors and filling out government forms. They live with the grace of those following natural orders and they know exactly how to do what they do; nobody asks them, at the last minute, to make a speech at the PTA meeting; no one expects them to understand the new software. It comforts us to consider the strong, smooth lines of their lives.

Unless we live in tall city apartment buildings, we catch an occasional glimpse of our local wildlife, though mostly, alas, flattened in the middle of the road. When we do see them alive, a deer on the lawn, raccoons or skunks foraging, we call our family in hushed tones to come and look, as we certainly wouldn't if the neighbor's dog were working on the garbage-can again. These are independent creatures sharing our world, and the thought is curiously pleasant, even comforting; we have company here.

Last winter a bear mauled the garbage on my back porch. I didn't see him, but gazing on his footprints and droppings I was awed and excited to know he was out there somewhere in the dark, a Martian visitor to my woods.

Now that we've mostly eliminated large, potentially dangerous, or dietarily competitive animals from our landscape, we have to take them on trust. Their existence, like that of extraterrestrials, has a vaguely mythic aura. We know them by their wall-calendars, by picture books and television specials, and we can go to the zoo and look at a representative of their kind, a sample tiger or sample gazelle, symbolic of presumed wild tigers and gazelles, but their separate, faraway, flesh-and-blood life in their own world takes a leap of faith.

As with extraterrestrials, we want to believe. We re-create them in the mind; set up, say, a tiger shouldering through dappled jungle shadows on his big silent feet, and hold him there until he's real, and suck some spiritual nourishment from the company of his foreignness.

If we were rich we could go on safari and see for ourselves, but so many people are there on the same errand, and the game-parks seem so much like oversized zoos, that it might feel more like a tour of the Disney back lot. We might as well content ourselves with the possibly fabulous beasts in the country of the mind. We might as well sit still and let our thoughts rest for a minute on a grizzly hooking for salmon in the Arctic, or a tortoise warming its cold blood on an empty beach, or wolf cubs wrestling, or the peculiar floating lurch of giraffes on the run.

They just might be real. We hope they're real. In case they are, we keep sending money to all those groups trying to hold off their extinction, at least for our lifetime, because when word finally does get back to us that the last wild animals are gone, we really will be alone here, and our thoughts will be hard-pressed for company. Nobody left but ourselves, and the thin hope of extraterrestrials who, if we're lucky, will now come roaring down from the skies like Noah and bring us two of each with which to start over.

Being Pregnant

BEING pregnant is fun because you needn't accomplish anything *else* today. No matter how many hours you frittered away with nothing concrete to show for them — no novels written, fortunes earned, trees planted, drowning swimmers resuscitated, cathedrals designed, or even missing buttons replaced — or even *dishes washed* — you were pregnant all day long. You were adding extra cells, maybe frivolous refinements like ears and fingernails, to a human body. That's enough to keep anyone busy and justify the day.

If you're into self-tending, you can concentrate on the self with an intensity that would be shameful otherwise. Count up your servings of fruits and vegetables, measure your intake of beta carotene, and shiver with delicious guilt at having been in the same room with a glass of wine. A generation ago, pregnancy was considered a fairly ordinary state, and the gravid could go through their days in much the usual way, but nowadays hundreds of warnings and restrictions call for nonstop concentration on the matter — an inadvertent lungful of the wrong air and you've ruined a human life forever.

This is a nuisance, but it does make you feel important.

Your once ordinary flesh has been elevated, almost sanctified. Friends and relations take an interest in it. You are making a person — an activity that anxious demographers feel has been overindulged in; there are already quite enough persons and then some, they tell us. However, demographers are necessarily concerned with quantity rather than quality and can't know that the particular person you're making will be such an improvement over the usual standard that its creation is not only essential, it may be crucial.

In addition, being pregnant enables you to feel gently, indulgently superior to the men in your life: no man has been known to create a new person since God modeled Eve out of whatsisname's rib. (The father of the fetus can draw an equally ancient and universal pleasure from knowing that his genetic luggage is being handed down, as important to the human male as to billy goat and tomcat, but somehow this seems a more abstract, less sensuous joy.)

Last but not least, pregnancy usually leads to a baby, and babies, especially for parents of a larky, lazy, easygoing temperament, are almost the best toy of all.

Babies

BEFORE the discovery of the psyche, raising babies was considered a skill well within reach of the amateur. Parents hugged, spanked, tickled, and scolded their offspring until they got too big; after that they considered the job at an end. Then Freud appeared.

Many of us grew up in the psychoanalytic decades, when it was correct and fashionable to blame mothers for all the peculiar tics of the adult human, from ailurophobia to promiscuity. Currently the guilt is spread more evenly around the home, and millions worship at support groups formed for the purpose of blaming one's whole birth family for abuse of one's inner child.

Not surprisingly, today's amateur parent approaches the job

anxiously, armed with threatening books and buttressed by professional counselors. Many have postponed the task almost to its natural limits while climbing the corporate ladder, and as a result they're not only less agile at chasing toddlers, less brisk at the office after a night of colic, they're more easily awed by the long-awaited responsibility. Raising children, once rather a jolly romp, is now a minefield. We hold their frail futures, vulnerable as a pulsing fontanel, in our clumsy hands.

True, we now deliver many of the parental rituals — decorating their birthday cakes, divulging the facts of life, teaching them to drive and throw a baseball, suggesting careers — into the hands of credentialed strangers, which is just as well, since who has the time these days? Besides, that's not *our* clutch on which they're learning to switch gears. Psychologically, though, we remain in the line of fire: all parents are potential villains. Our lightest word may launch them into a lifetime of costly therapy.

Actually, this is horsefeathers, as experienced parents discover. Anyone who has raised more than one child knows full well that kids turn out the way they turn out — astonishingly, for the most part, and usually quite unlike their siblings, even their twins, raised under the same flawed rooftree. Little we have done or said, or left undone and unsaid, seems to have made much mark. It's hubris to suppose ourselves so influential; a casual remark on the playground is as likely to change their lives as any dedicated campaign of ours. They come with much of their own software already in place, waiting, and none of the keys we press will override it.

Of course, if they do turn out to be sweet-natured, cheerful, healthy, loving, responsible, good-looking rocket scientists, we're allowed to take a modest bow, but the truth is we had precious little to do with it, any more than we did with their siblings who now languish in prison for chain-saw murders. We might as well lean back and enjoy them.

While they're very small, they're warm and cuddly and usually rather smelly; they burp and drool; their heads loll and their eyes drift. At this stage, only the most sentimental can find much fun in them. It passes quickly, though, and they learn to focus, smile, and brandish their fists comically. Now we can put funny hats on them and take pictures. Give them a kitchen spoon and a pot to bang on. Drag them out of their cribs and show them off to our friends, who can pass them from hand to hand and teach them to make rude noises. Presently they learn to walk, staggering amusingly around the room and crowing with contagious delight. They learn to talk, and sometimes get off magnificently witty *mots* we can repeat to all and sundry.

As they get older, they give us cause to play with electric trains, go to the zoo, the park, the circus, and the Fourth of July parade, build a snowman, reread *Charlotte's Web,* and experience such modern wonders as Nintendo and the Super Soaker. (Having a child around is more fun than being one, since we're free to leave the small world for the large one whenever we get bored.) The childless, however they may secretly long for roller-coaster rides and the smell of cotton candy, would be embarrassed to indulge themselves, and no dignified, responsible adult can be seen throwing snowballs in his front yard unless there's a child in evidence.

We can invest in computer games to play with, on the pretext that they improve junior's eye-hand coordination; we can take him to frivolous movies; we can spend an extra week lolling around at the beach because junior needs the fresh air.

We can also hope that, when we reel into our dotage, instead of setting us adrift on an ice floe they'll sing to us, comb our hair, spoon in our gruel, and maybe read us *Charlotte's Web.*

Growing Up

THE first ten or twelve years are just one triumph after another, and the giddy glow of accomplishment lights up our ambitions for the rest of our lives, even if our later achievements are always a little ambiguous, a little clouded, compared with the ringing clarity of learning to climb stairs, flip a light-switch, or ride a two-wheeler.

It's a good thing life starts out so well; we need the reserves of optimism later. Early on, the lessons are so clear-cut that success is almost automatic, and power piles on power. We learn to talk. We point and say "Want dat!" and, miraculously, someone gives it to us. We learn to crawl to a destination under our own steam without waiting to be carried. Less easily, because it's such a recent, artificial concept, we learn to use the toilet and are rewarded by the absence of diapers, which were grossly uncomfortable. Then we can reach the doorknob. Tie our shoes. Turn on the television. Print our names. Tell time. Button our shirts. Read, roller-skate, play checkers, throw a ball, spend money, and find our way around the once menacing corridors of school.

By ten or twelve we balance on a pinnacle of achievement we will never even glimpse again; monarchs of all we survey, *we can do everything there is to do.* We are king of the kids, and can bully or instruct the lesser kids at will.

The fall, when it comes, is awful, and best forgotten. From being foremost among the kids, overnight we become the least and lowliest of adolescents. All our accomplishments turn to ashes; it no longer counts that we can ride no-hands and whistle through our fingers. The new lessons are murky ones and the new triumphs shaky. The first kiss may be a thrill but shadows of insecurity surround it. The first menstruation is messy and embarrassing. Being picked to play on the varsity invokes the possibility of failure and public disgrace; first sex is notoriously awkward. Learning to drive promises a surge of power but delivers more traffic-jams than joy. And all the social and romantic skills we need are slow in coming and somehow never fall into place with the fail-safe, permanent click of learning how to hang by our knees.

Still, the early years shore most of us up through the tasks of the teens, and we stagger out the far end into the light of independence. This is fine. We can stay up all night and eat cold pizza for breakfast. We can get credit cards and buy our own toys. We can take up with unsuitable friends and lovers and use bad words, or even bad grammar. No one can make us go to school, or wear a raincoat, or clean up our room, or remember to say thank you, or kiss Aunt Doris, or wash our hands, or be nice to our sister, or put away our toys, or hang up our jacket, or eat our turnips, or respect our elders.

For a while there, it's glorious. Not quite as glorious as being ten, because we do have to pay the electric bill and get to work on time, but glorious enough.

Then most of us marry and find that somehow, mysteriously, we once again have to say thank you and hang up our jackets, but it was grand while it lasted.

Getting Older

THERE'S a lot to be said for being twenty, and many of us try to prolong this expectant springtime state for decades, partly because we think the younger we look the more fun we will have, and partly because the human animal ages less handsomely than the rest of the world; your elderly dog may be stout and arthritic but she doesn't need a face-lift. Still, getting older, a gradual process measured by various milestones, has joys of its own and, as is often said, beats the alternative. There are those who feel that, after a certain point, getting younger would be nice, but if we did we'd miss our dear friends heading in the opposite direction on the other escalator.

At twenty, much of what we did, or felt we ought to do, was educational; we were studying for the career of being adults. We thought we needed opinions on everything, because we still thought our opinions would matter and people were going to listen to them. We prepared ourselves to argue everything — French film directors, how long to cook pasta, energy alternatives, psychology, Surrealism, relativity. It was hard work, and ten years later we realized nobody cared what we thought. Nobody even cared whether or not we'd read Henry James.

This is a blow at first, but once accepted it's very relaxing. If we're mathematically illiterate, so be it. If we don't appreciate postmodern architecture, even our loved ones will stop trying to convert us. It we didn't master German irregular verbs at twenty, by forty we can tell ourselves it no longer matters much, and at the rate we're going we'll never get to the castles on the Rhine anyway. Those who read the first fifty pages of *War and Peace* half-a-dozen times may now shrug, sigh, and take the matchbook out of page fifty: we were planning to become the sort of person who'd read *War and Peace*, but we're no longer in the state of becoming; we already are, and it is, happily, too late.

Suddenly — we must have blinked — the finals are over, the grades are in, and we are who we are. We're dismissed. Free to do and read and see and listen to what pleases us, quite reckless of its educational necessity or political correctness.

We can drop back from the vanguard. If there's an exhibition of scrap metal welded into chunks called *Orgasm (Blue)* or *Infinity IV*, we needn't go. If we do go, we needn't pretend we found it challenging. Ignoring challenge is one of the happier perks.

Educationally speaking, we can loosen our tie and put our feet up. We can take out the mental toys we did manage to acquire and play with them. We can beat our cultural swords into plowshares.

After certain milestones are passed, we no longer expect ourselves to keep up with the times. At twenty, it's disgraceful not to understand quarks or the VCR; at forty it's perfectly acceptable. (If we do understand them we may even be accused of not acting our age, as if we were wearing a bikini in public.) Pleasantly, most of our friends have also grown older at about the same rate of speed and don't understand quarks either, so we needn't feel ignorant.

It was a strain, first preparing ourselves to be perfect people and then racing full tilt to stay perfect. Now, unpressured, we can sink into the timeless backwaters — bridge, botany, Greek, needlepoint, Civil War biographies, golf. Forgive ourselves for all we have failed to achieve.

The burdens of guilt grow lighter with age; we spent decades smiting our brows for real or imagined crimes and what good has it done? We might as well forget it.

Social embarrassments, so shattering at twenty, fade too. The first time we can duck into a store or restaurant and use the bathroom without having to buy something, pretending the purchase was why we came, is a satisfying milestone in adulthood. No longer do we wake writhing in shame when we remember the afternoon we spent, all unaware, with a bit of salad between our front teeth or catsup on our shirt. The world will have to accept us for what we have become. Quite likely the world wasn't even watching; invisibility settles over the middle-aged, and this is relaxing and brings us exciting chances to eavesdrop unnoticed on strangers, not to mention the joy of wearing comfortable shoes.

When we get even older, we'll be allowed to take naps and tell the same stories over and over again.

Unless, of course, our face-lift was so successful that everyone thinks we're twenty and ought to be reading *War and Peace*.

The Songs of Our Youth

THE songs we listened to during certain years of our lives — from age twelve to twenty-two, maybe — are the songs that will ring in the dark, interior coils of our ears until we die. We don't add new songs and forget the old. Our eyes adjust to the way the world changes, and this year's skirt-length quickly comes to seem more attractive than last year's, but our ears never adjust.

Mostly we march along hand in hand with popular culture, adopting its new tastes in movie stars and hair-styles and wondering how we could ever have worn such clothes or laughed at such jokes or eaten such tuna casseroles, but our ears stand still. They've snapped shut like an oyster around the songs of our youth, never to replace or mislay them, quite regardless of any possible lyrical or musical merit.

These songs are nontransferable. They belong to our generation; like wars and assassinations, they're part of what makes us sisters

and brothers to everyone else our age. We can read our children the
books we loved as children, and our children love them too, but
play them Simon and Garfunkel, the Beatles, Rosemary Clooney,
Frank Sinatra, and they gaze at us in despair and bewilderment as
if we'd turned to stone before their eyes. It's the first great disillu-
sionment of the young with their parents, and vice versa: their
appallingly awful taste in popular music.

A radio station can figure the precise age of its listeners, or the
listeners it would like to lure, and know precisely what to play for
them. If the station chooses, in defiance of its advertising clients, to
grow old along with its audience, it can go on playing the same
songs over and over until the last graybeard listener keels over,
smiling, to Fred Astaire singing "Cheek to Cheek," the final, incor-
ruptible fragment of his youth like a pearl in his dying ear.

Wave after wave of generations march toward the cliff, each to
its own tunes — Bing Crosby, Dick Haymes, Judy Garland, Mar-
garet Whiting. Elvis Presley, Patsy Cline, the Grateful Dead, the
Doors, Michael Jackson. . . .

In an age of fraying community, they're community, our lingua
franca. They're democracy itself, ignoring our race, creed, intelligence, taste, and socioeconomic class: admission is solely by age-
bracket.

They feel exactly right, these songs, in our heads and on our
tongues. They fit us as familiarly as our bedroom slippers, but
they're less scruffy. In fact, they shine. They glitter all over with
jewels like the blue convertible of our seventeenth year that had to

be jump-started daily and the love, real or imagined, that burned like a coal in the breast.

Unlike the general ruck of souvenirs, their shelf-life is limitless. Your sentimental mother may have saved your prom dress in a chest, full repulsive in turquoise satin with flounces; you may have saved mawkish love-letters lumpy with clichés; you blush for shame, but let the band strike up "Begin the Beguine" or "Rock Around the Clock" or whatever it was, and you're there. The time is now and the night is young, no matter how old it's grown.

Listen, the graying couple whispers, reaching for each other's hands: they're playing our song.

They're a happy cargo to carry around, these songs, weightless, taking up no space in our suitcases, always fresh and available. A few whistled or murmured bars rejuvenate the soul. And one of these days we can turn our old heads to a neighbor in the geriatric ward and say, "Remember Pete Seeger? Sarah Vaughan? Arlo Guthrie? Hank Williams? Do you know the words to 'Scarborough Fair'? 'Strawberry Fields'? 'Send in the Clowns'?"

And our grizzled neighbor — compatriot, kinsman — will hang fire for a moment, groping, and then begin to croak something that's almost a recognizable tune, and we can join in. Maybe the whole toothless ward of us will starting singing, pounding out the beat with spoons on bedpans, cackling with remembered joys, as time sweeps us toward the cliffs.

Cattle

BRITISH pastoral romantics make a great fuss about cows, claiming that just to look at a cow makes them feel good all over, but actually cows are an anxious, neurotic lot, living to produce milk and more cows, and their friendship with humans has always been dicey. Cows are rather like the misogynistic view of women generally, being perpetually touchy and reproductive.

Meat cattle are different. Around population centers, you see them in transitional rural areas where the original farmer has gratefully sold off his arduous acres to a nonfarmer who likes the ambience of a farm but doesn't want to go out in the broiling sun to plow or get up in the dark to milk. He wants to go into the city and be a lawyer instead, so he fattens beef cattle. It isn't strenuous. In the spring a truck comes and drops off a bunch of scenic young steers, and in the fall the same truck comes back and collects the now much larger bovines and takes them away to fuel the McDonald'ses and Burger Kings of the world. The lawyer's only contribution has been paying the negligible agricultural taxes on the acreage and inviting his friends to bring their drinks out to the patio and admire his farm.

All summer, the future hamburgers amble through the pleasant fields and wade in the pond. Stand together in the sprawling shade of the pasture tree. If you're walking by, they come to the fence. They like people. Big as a Buick, calm as a clam, the steer leans his chin on the top rail and asks to be rubbed right there, in the short crisp curls of his broad, bony forehead. His eyes are enormous and blankly soulful. He smells of grass. Others crowd around. They all want their foreheads rubbed.

Later, in November, when you go by the field is empty. But people like hamburgers, and if they didn't, the big sweet-smelling fellows, not being household pets, would never have lived at all to spend such a pleasant summer in such a green field. The quality of life is not measured in years, and of course the steer has what Tennessee Williams called the pig's advantage: no premonition in the summer's field of the winter's Big Macs. Rather a pity we can't all buy into that, but worth keeping in mind.

Carpe diem.

Books

I HAVE been told, repeatedly, that ten minutes of prayer a day can increase my annual income by an average of fifteen to twenty percent. Being lazy and scatterbrained, I've never buckled down to this regimen, but now I hear that reading — "Read to Succeed!" — can have the same effect, and here I may have better luck.

Books, it turns out, have a solid practical value convertible into coin of the realm and improved business management, interpersonal relations, and mental health. This has made a useful occupation out of what had been just a primitive form of entertainment. Children are being urged to read, not for joy but for profit.

Still, there are books, other books, that will never lead to success but that provide an odd, separate, impractical pleasure not offered by anything else on earth. I don't mean noble ideas or philosophical insights, since I seem to be immune to them both, but the books that move permanently into one's head and construct their own space there, a kind of walled garden full of tame dragons, that we can walk around in whenever we want. Since this is probably the most threatened of all our old joys, surviving only in isolated pockets of the population and no longer known to breed, it needs explaining.

The habit began in childhood, before electronic amusements wiped out boredom. Some children may have been perfectly satisfied with their actual lives, but others found them a grinding agony of tedium and learned early how to slip out of them and into a book. From here it was a simple step to carrying the book around with them, invisibly, in the head. The teacher droned on, the child felt his eyes lock and glaze over and himself begin to vaporize. He might struggle to hang on to reality, but it was no use; in a matter of minutes his essence was sucked from him and remolded into Huck on the river, Kim on the Grand Trunk Road, Jim Hawkins on the *Hispaniola*, leaving but an empty husk at his desk. (There was no use trying to teach fractions to this husk, of course, and it was no way to get ahead in school or anywhere else; it's criminal to tell children that reading leads to success.)

In a more sociable vein, children as late as the 1960s would "play" a book together, as in, "Let's play 'Alice.' I'll be Alice and you can be the Dormouse." "No, I'll be the Queen and chop off your head."

We got older and seized some control over our inner lives and learned to stay within our flesh when need be, but at the same time we'd been reading more books. Whole colonies of books. Parts of the head became perfect honeycombs of books.

Certain works set up housekeeping in us more physically than others. This had less to do with literary quality than with the construction of a quirky, self-contained world operating under its own odd logic, an independent world that could be snipped loose from ordinary time and place and stowed neatly in the head: *Pickwick Papers*, for instance, in contrast to the rest of Dickens; *Cannery Row* in contrast to the rest of Steinbeck. From *The Wind in the Willows* to *The Lord of the Rings* to *Wuthering Heights*, they carried around their own portable geography.

A lot of these works are British. I don't know why this should be so, unless claustrophobia inspires people to build on extra rooms. Perhaps on a crowded island with a doleful climate it's natural to construct *Green Mansions* and *Robinson Crusoe* and *A High Wind in Jamaica*. Maybe in America, the West has been our novel; maybe the Oregon Trail was quirky and self-referential enough to satisfy the urge. (American southerners, though, like Faulkner and Welty and O'Connor and McCullers, seemed to actually live in their self-sealing fictional places; presumably they got mail, answered the phone, and turned on the television news there, just as if the game were real.)

Book by book the worlds accreted. Maybe they're not walled gardens at all — that would be far too many gardens. Maybe this is a long, narrow corridor lined with doors, and each door bears a small brass plate saying, for instance, "*Out of Africa* by Isak Dinesen," and we can choose and open any door we want. It isn't even necessary to find and reread the book. We only need to say its name and the door swings.

There's the movie, someone says. Why waste time with the book in the first place when we can rent the movie at the nearest video store and see the whole thing in a couple of hours without the effort of reading?

Well, yes and no. Movies somehow don't occupy the same kind of space. Someone else's hands have made them visible. Forced the pictures on us. The film vision is thrust in through the fronts of our eyes, while the book vision rises up naturally behind them, organically, so to speak, out of our personal, dark, mossy convolutions, and this seems to make all the difference. The movie's not ours. We can't tamper with it, can't even replace Merle Oberon as an unsatisfactory Cathy, because a movie exists outside our heads. To watch the movie of a loved book devastates the interior landscape, pushes the hills and trees around and muddles the faces. (Disney movies of the great children's books are particularly intrusive, and have left more than one classic an abandoned ruin, haunted only by tap-dancing buzzards with long eyelashes.)

Sometimes a television series creates one of these habitable alternative universes — *The Waltons*, maybe, or *Star Trek* — but their citizens on the screen are so physically explicit that it's hard to daydream one's way into their flesh. The scenery has already been built and the furnishings invented; we can't make our own.

No, the rooms along the corridor are reserved for books, and only certain books at that. And, like our songs, they're portable and permanent. Let the house burn to the ground, let friends, family, hair, and teeth desert us, let us be chained to the dripping wall of a dungeon in utter darkness, and still the door will open when we name it.

I expect this to be a great satisfaction to me when I'm blind and bedridden, with tubes poking out from every orifice. I shall whisper silently, "*The Sword in the Stone,*" and the door will open on Merlin the magician with his owl, Archimedes, perched on his shoulder making messes down his back. "Wash up," Merlin tells the breakfast dishes, and they scamper into the dishwater squealing and splashing each other.

Except for an occasional alcohol rub, I suppose this will be my last earthly pleasure. I hope there'll be doors enough to see me out. And maybe, if I'm lucky, I'll simply disappear through one of them in the end, like the schoolboy sucked away from his desk, and find myself not in hell or heaven but on the Grand Trunk Road, wearing Kim's dusty rags and merrily stealing sweetmeats for my lama.